The Perfect Enough

COMPANION BOOK

ACHIEVING HAPPINESS AND BALANCE WITH

THE DISCOVER PROCESS

LAURA KING

Summit PRESS

1375 N. Killian Drive
Lake Park, FL 33403
877.482.7352
www.summitpress.net

Perfect Enough Companion Book

Published by
Summit Press
1375 N. Killian Drive
Lake Park, FL 33403
877-482-7352

To buy books in quantity for
corporate use or incentives,
call (877) 482-7352 or email
laurakinginfo@gmail.com

Credits:
Layout: Jonathan Gullery / RJ Communications

Cover Design: Timothy J. Paul * Highlan Design *
highlandesign@yahoo.com

Photographer: Allan Carlisle Photography

International Standard Book Number (ISBN) 978-0-9792996-1-2
Library of Congress Control Number: 2007929436
Printed in the United States of America
1st printing

At the Summit Hypnosis Centers, I use the **DISCOVER PROCESS** for outcome creation, planning, and achievement (i.e., what most people refer to as goal setting). It's simple, it's easy to remember, and you can do it yourself in the privacy and comfort of your own home. The **DISCOVER PROCESS** takes advantage of the ability of hypnosis to turn suggestions into behavior, and NLP's program for manifesting the outcomes you desire. This is where we integrate hypnosis, NLP, and your own unique abilities and wishes, and produce what you have defined for yourself as happiness and balance.

Here's to achieving your ideal life!

Much love,
Laura

CONTENTS

Section A

Section B

SECTION A

THE POWER OF THE COMPANION BOOK

The Perfect Enough Companion Book walks you through the **DISCOVER PROCESS**, which helps you create new maps for your subconscious so you can achieve the happiness and balance you deserve. Though it can be used by itself, it's most helpful when used in conjunction with Perfect Enough. By examining your fears and your past experiences and learning how to let go of the both, you create the space for a new way of thinking about your life. You create the space for your new map, and you literally write the scripts for your future. This is the power of the Companion Book: the power to design and manifest your future.

It's my wish for you that you are able to reach inside yourself to access your capacity for boundless peace and joy. We all have it, but through our life's trials and tribulations, and our perceptions of them, we lose our vitality and our confidence in our potential. We forget that we can have everything we desire and that we're entitled to happiness, health, and success in all endeavors. Whether your main purpose is to be the best parent, spouse, or child, or the best salesperson at your company, it doesn't matter. Your approach will be the same. You can find the strength to be the best you can be no matter what area of life you choose to work on. Completing the entire **DISCOVER PROCESS,** accurately and with intention, will activate your life personally, financially, and spiritually.

THE *DISCOVER PROCESS* DEFINED

The **DISCOVER PROCESS** takes you from your decision that your life could use some enhancing, all the way through to the manifestation of what you used to think of as impossible dreams. As you go through the 8 Keys, you'll do the following:

D   Decide to Change
I   Identify Your Fears
S   Self-Inquiry
C   Conscious-Level Action Steps
O   Outcome Development Board
V   Visualize, with the Help of Hypnosis
E   Evaluate Your Progress
R   Revise & Repeat

D=Decide to Change

Though deciding to change your behavior is a necessary first step, the actual change requires more than just the decision. A perfect example is what most people do with New Year's resolutions. Once a year, with enthusiasm and confidence, many people proclaim: "This year, I'm going to be a more positive person," or, "This is the year I'm going to treat my body better and lose those 20 pounds." They claim that acknowledging that they need to change is the first step toward achieving their goals. And that's true. But by February 1, most New Year's resolutions are distant memories, and precious little progress has been achieved toward goals that were supposed to be of the utmost importance.

GOING TO SEMINARS AND
BUYING CASSETTES AND CDS IS NOT ENOUGH

For many people, once they realize they need some help to get over their past mistakes and achieve what they are capable of, they go to a seminar and/or order some self-help tapes. They jump up and down, clap, and cheer enthusiastically at the seminar, then listen to the tapes everyday for a week or two. Soon the excitement of their personal potential wears off and, well, they're back to where they started.

WHAT'S MISSING? WHAT'S THE SECRET INGREDIENT?

Actually, there are three secret ingredients, and they work together:

1.   using the subconscious to deliver your goals,
2.   practicing your desired positive behavior, and
3.   practicing your desired mental behavior (i.e., your thought patterns).

After all, what keeps many people from accomplishing their goals can usually be distilled down to one simple concept: their behavior doesn't support their goal.

What do you do when you learn new yoga postures? You practice them until you get them right, of course. What eludes most people is that changing the way we approach our thoughts should be handled in the same way. So if you feel like you beat yourself up over past mistakes and you want to change that thought-behavior, you'll be much more successful if you practice, practice, practice.

Fortunately, peak personal performance is a learned ability. It can be reached on a consistent basis if you are able to cancel negative thought patterns. Peak performance isn't about luck, and it won't occur with just talent and practice. Your mind must be engaged and actively monitoring whether how you're feeling and thinking in a particular moment needs to be changed. And if change is necessary, your mind must be trained to swiftly, effectively alter your thoughts and feelings.

The successful person recommends this approach: If you've done something in the past that you feel you can and should change, then by all means take action. If you've been unkind to someone, apologize to them. If you failed to fulfill a promise you made, take steps to fulfill that promise. If you made a mistake in a relationship, devote more of your time to whatever it was you had difficulty with in that relationship. If you've succeeded at something in the past, recall that success and model it.

The unsuccessful person wallows in regret and self-pity over anything negative and uses language that furthers the depth of their misery. Naturally, the unsuccessful person is then unable to move forward. The strategy of berating yourself for past conduct solves nothing and only serves to lower your self-esteem. You create a vicious cycle where negative experiences and negative feelings are reinforced, which leads to more negative outcomes and more negative feelings.

You aren't going to change one bit of your past. What's done is done. Learn from your past experiences and move on. You did the best you could, given your awareness and understanding of your options at the time. You are human and it is in our nature to make mistakes. You have nothing to gain from self-condemnation except feelings of misery and inadequacy.

I'll provide you with a space specifically for your affirmation of your decision to change in each Key.

I =Identify Your Fears

You might think that I'm going to help you eliminate your fear, but actually there's no such thing. Instead, we aim for mastery of fear. As Mark Twain once said, "Courage is resistance to and mastery of fear—not the absence of fear." In order to master your fear, you must identify it and get to know it well. Is it rational? Irrational? Either way, it is real to you in your mind. If you acknowledge the origin as irrational, it might become easier to overcome. But it might not. So always treat all fear with equal respect.

After you've identified your fear, you must name it and write its biography. This is what I call a fear profile: the history of your fear. When did it come into your life? Why? Describe the day, if you recall, and/or the circumstance. Like when you are doing a Theater of the Mind exercise, compose a story with rich sensory details. Often the mere creation and writing of the story deepens your understanding of your fear and helps you master it. Remember, you cannot master something if you don't know it well.

Our fears are what hold us back from living a happy and balanced life. Though fear is a painful emotion that may or may not be related to something real or rational, because the subconscious cannot differentiate between what's real and what's imaginary, fear affects your life as soon as it enters it (that is, as soon as you allow it to enter as fear). And the more attention you give it, the more life it takes on.

Fear is your mind's way of making a potentially embarrassing or uncomfortable situation seem greater than it really is. Essentially, fear makes mountains out of molehills, and prevents us from enjoying our lives. You may have even heard FEAR defined as False Evidence Appearing Real. For example, the most common fear is of public speaking. It's more common than the fear of death (which, in case you were wondering, weighs in at #7). This is a perfect example of how irrational fear can be. Let's say you are indeed afraid of public speaking. What exactly is it that you are afraid of? Is public speaking a life and death situation for you? For anyone? Are you likely to be physically hurt in any way as a result of public speaking, even if you're terrible at it? No.

I'll provide you with a space to list your fears for each Key.

S=Self-Inquiry

Visualizing and thinking about past successes is an excellent way to build confidence and self-esteem. What you think about is what you become. Therefore, when you concentrate on your successes, you help to create future successes. *What are some of your successes?*

I'll provide you with a space to list your successes in each Key.

C=Conscious-Level Action Steps

In each of the 8 Keys, after you've identified your fears and written their profiles, you'll be presented with various exercises that work on the conscious level to help you master and release your fears, and replace them with notions that encourage happiness and balance. Some exercises are unique to a particular Key, but here are some that can be used with all of them:

• BREATHWORK

The in-breath followed by the out-breath represents tension and release. And when the breath is blocked, the body and mind are blocked and in a state of substandard performance. There must be freely flowing breath in order for there to be peak performance. When you disconnect from your breath, you prevent flow, and you get lost on your way to the zone.

• BLOWING YOUR FEARS AWAY

Find a quiet place and breathe deeply, slowly, and completely. Visualize the thing, event, or person that is at the center of your biggest fear. See everything about the moment you fear most, then add more sensory details. Feel that moment of your biggest fear. Smell it. Hear it.

Then . . . shrink it. Continue to shrink the picture in your mind until it is so small that when you hold it in the palm of your hand you can barely see, feel, smell, or hear it. Then . . . blow on it once, and send it off into oblivion, never to return.

• MODELING

Each Key requires you to imagine someone or something that is the embodiment of what you'd like to become. For example, Bill Gates is my model for Meaning. I use the Theater of the Mind to visualize Bill Gates and how he acts and reacts, and how people feel when they stand next to him, and then I transfer those feelings to myself. I become the embodiment of the wonderful qualities of Bill Gates.

I'll provide you with space to record your thoughts and feelings regarding your conscious-level work in each Key.

O=Outcome Development Board

Once you have a model of whatever it is you'd like to achieve, your next step is to find images, photos, and words that reflect your outcome, and paste them onto the appropriate section of the Outcome Board that comes with your Perfect Enough Toolkit (or the poster you create on your own). This vital step will help train your brain to create your goal-images. Manifesting your future becomes as easy as looking at your board and doing your self-hypnosis. Your outcome board is the final step you can take, on the conscious level, to create a life of happiness and balance. Cut out and paste photos and words that represent your model of whatever the Key represents, as well as your past successes regarding the Key. Your objective is to create a story on your board of what you want your outcomes to be and you can tell a story, beginning with "I am….".

I'll provide you with space to explore your thoughts and feelings about your outcome board in each key.

V=Visualize, with the Help of Hypnosis

This is where you enlist your powerful subconscious mind to help you manifest the future you desire. After you take yourself into Alpha using Instant Alpha Conditioning, you'll use visualization to help you become more confident, persistent, loving, and healthy. Your powers of visualization will increase your prosperity and your happiness, and do it much faster than anything you can do on the conscious level alone.

THE POWER OF COMPOUNDING

In each of the Keys to the **DISCOVER PROCESS**, you'll have opportunities to use your subconscious to create balance and happiness in your life. Each of the eight sessions is associated with a letter in DISCOVER. This technique is called compounding, the effect of which is that each time you see, hear, or say the word DISCOVER, all of the effects of your sessions are triggered and made exponentially more powerful. You need to remember the word DISCOVER at least once every 36 hours to get the full effect. It's like a mathematical equation: each time you see or say DISCOVER, the effect of this program gets stronger and stronger. At the end of each script for the Keys, you'll notice a sentence that looks something like this:

This entire suggestion is represented by the letter "D" of my sub-key word "Discover." Anytime I think, say, or see the word "Discover," all suggestions keyed to this word are automatically activated, stimulated and work for my benefit.

E=Evaluate Your Progress

Each Key requires attention each night for at least three weeks. And there are 8 Keys. That means if you do the **DISCOVER PROCESS** *continuously, it will take 24 weeks--about six months--to complete it. At the end of your six months, I recommend you revisit each Key and ask yourself: Have I achieved my goal/ outcome for this Key?*

R=Revise & Repeat

When you evaluate your progress, you'll find that you've developed strengths in areas where you were once weak, and that some of your goals have been achieved. I'll provide you with DISCOVER Flash Cards with affirmations on them to reinforce your progress in each Key.

I recommend that regardless of whether you've achieved your goals, you repeat the entire **DISCOVER PROCESS** for another six months. Reaffirm your strengths, and confirm your outcomes. Tweak your affirmations to reflect that you have already been successful and will continue to be successful. And above all, never stop using your mind to create your best life.

SECTION B

KEY 1

SELF-CONFIDENCE

FROM INSECURE TO EMPOWERED

"I was always looking outside myself for strength and confidence but it comes from within. It is there all the time." —Anna Freud

When you walk into a room, do you feel like you're in charge? Do you feel confident? When you speak, do people listen? If not, it is time to figure out why and to move from insecure to empowered using the **DISCOVER PROCESS**.

D=Decide to Change

If your self-confidence is not at a level that makes you feel like you can do *anything*, your first step is to decide to do something about it, and acknowledge that you'd like to move from insecure to empowered. In this space provided, write about your decision to change the status of your self-confidence. Begin with some form of the following affirmation: *I acknowledge that I am Perfect Enough and I recognize and embrace this opportunity to enhance my self-confidence.*

_____

_____

_____

_____

_____

_____

_____

I=Identify Your Fears

What is creating your feelings of insecurity? What are you afraid of? List your fears, giving each one a name. Describe the day of birth, if you recall, and/or the circumstance that brought the above fears into your life. Like when you are doing a Theater of the Mind exercise, compose a story with rich sensory details. Often the mere creation and writing of the story deepens your understanding of your fear and helps you master it. Remember, you cannot master something if you don't know it well.

_____

_____

_____

_____

_____

_____

_____

_____

_____

S=Self-Inquiry

Visualizing and thinking about past successes is an excellent way to build confidence and self-esteem. What you think about is what you become. Therefore, when you concentrate on your successes, you help to create future successes. *What are some of your successes?*

_____

_____

_____

_____

_____

_____

_____

_____

_____

_____

Take time each day to remind yourself of all of the things you're good at, and all of the ways you are improving and growing as a person (and mother, daughter, father, son, employer, employee, community member). Remind yourself of all the positive experiences you have had and all the successes you have achieved. Tell yourself that you are brave, smart, balanced, and confident. Tell yourself that you are proud of your achievements and that you believe in your abilities. And, most important of all, remind yourself that each mistake you've made along the way has been a learning experience that has brought you to where you are today.

When you do something well, tell yourself, out loud, "I did that well." And when you make a mistake, make sure you look for the things you did well or correctly. Do whatever it is you're doing, the best way you can, while being the best person you can be. Expect you can learn and do as well as anyone by getting rid of everything that blocks you mentally, emotionally, and physically (unchecked mental and emotional issues inevitably manifest as physical problems). Tell yourself that you can overcome any obstacle, and recall all the times you overcame obstacles in the past. Congratulate yourself, and expect similar persistence and success in the present.

C=Conscious-Level Action Steps

TIPS FOR DEALING WITH A CRISIS IN SELF-CONFIDENCE

• INSTANT CHANGE OF STATE

The instant an unpleasant thought enters your mind simply assure yourself that "The most powerful experience of this moment is the relaxation I am feeling." When you say this, you are diminishing the power of the fear and its effect on you. You are taken to a place of safety and serenity so your body can use its precious resources productively rather than waste them on overreacting.

Face your fears slowly to desensitize yourself to their effects. And repeat your exposure to them over and over until you realize that the dread in your head is much greater than the actual potential for harm.

• BREATHWORK

The in-breath followed by the out-breath represents tension and release. And when the breath is blocked, the body and mind are blocked and in a state of substandard performance. There must be freely flowing breath in order for peak performance and true contentment to exist. When you disconnect from your breath, you prevent flow, and you get lost on your way to the zone. You create tension that is at cross-purposes with the balance and happiness you're working to achieve.

• BLOWING YOUR FEARS AWAY

Find a quiet place and breathe deeply, slowly, and completely. Visualize the thing, event, or person that is at the center of your biggest fear. See everything about the moment you fear most, then add more sensory details. Feel that moment of your biggest fear. Smell it. Hear it. Then . . . shrink it. Continue to shrink the image in your mind until it's so small that when you hold it in the palm of your hand you can barely see, feel, smell, or hear it. Then . . . blow on it once, and send it off into oblivion, never to return.

When you face your fears you quickly and easily move into the realm of security, trust, and confidence in your own abilities. And included in those abilities, is the capacity you have to change your life and reach your potential.

ACTION STEP
MODELING SELF-CONFIDENCE

- Who represents self-confidence to you?
- Close your eyes and imagine that person.
- Envision how the person stands, how they walk, and how they use their hands and eyes.
- Imagine that person interacting with others. What does their voice sound like? What do they look like when they're listening? Observe how the other people react to your confident person.
- Imagine yourself standing close to your confident person. How do you feel? Can you feel their confidence?
- Pretend you're a human sponge and soak up the self-confidence of your model.
- Turn to the people in your vision and watch them react to you the same way they reacted to your confident person. Feel their respect and admiration, and feel your charisma and confidence.
- Now, open your eyes.

What are your thoughts and feelings about your modeling experience?

_____

_____

_____

_____

_____

_____

_____

_____

_____

O =Outcome Development Board

Cut out and paste photos and words that represent your model of self-confidence, and words and images that represent your past success onto section #1 of your outcome board. You are creating a story with your board of what you want your outcomes to be, and you will begin that story with "I am…..".

Here are some tips for choosing the most effective images:
- Look for images of the body you would like to have, but keep it realistic for your height and body type.
- Look for pictures of people with the facial expressions and posture similar to the person you modeled in the modeling Action Step above.

- Look for pictures of people who are dressed in a way that represents self-confidence to you.
- Use your information from your self-inquiry.

What are your thoughts and feelings regarding your experience of completing this first section of your outcome board?

_____

_____

_____

_____

_____

_____

_____

_____

_____

_____

_____

_____

_____

_____

_____

V=Visualize, with the Help of Hypnosis

USE HYPNOSIS TO TURBO-CHARGE YOUR NEW SELF-CONFIDENCE

When you have a poor self-image, your first job is to recognize it. Then, in order to successfully develop a healthier, more positive self-image, you must release the negative one to make room for the new one. As with any self-hypnosis script, you must relax yourself first by using Instant Alpha Conditioning. Next, follow with the "Release and Clear" script to clear out negative thoughts, memories, or other images that creep into your mind and invade your thinking. This makes your brain available for more productive things. Once you have done the "Release and Clear" script 21 times, proceed to the "Self Confidence" script. *Remember to read the Instant Alpha Conditioning script before any self-hypnosis script.*

Let's get rid of your self-sabotaging thoughts and replace them with positive messages of Self-Confidence!

INSTANT ALPHA CONDITIONING

Instructions:

1. Use the word you selected to replace the longer Alpha conditioning script. Read the following script and let Alpha occur.
2. Proceed directly to the script for Release and Clear, and read each night, before retiring, for 21 nights. If you miss a night, you must begin again. Read aloud, with feeling.

S	M	T	W	Th	F	Sat

3. Say the words Release and Clear every night thereafter.

From this moment on, each and every time I desire to attain the deep state of total relaxation, I am instantly and fully relaxed, as I am now drifting into the Alpha state of consciousness. The moment I think my chosen word _____, Alpha occurs. This word has an effect only when I use it and only under the proper circumstances. Each and every time I do use it, I am fully prepared to receive positive, beneficial and constructive suggestions, impressing each one deeper into my storage and memory facility of my brain.

From this moment on, _____ triggers deep relaxation of my mind and body. I feel Alpha occur. I feel wonderful. I feel comfortable. I am totally receptive and responsive to my own creative ideas and suggestions. I am bathed in a glow of quietness, peace, and serenity. My chosen word works only when I deliberately use it for deep relaxation to attain Alpha consciousness. Its use in regular conversation has no effect on me whatsoever. From this moment on, each and every time I desire the deep state of total relaxation, I am instantly and fully relaxed upon saying _____. Because my subconscious must follow my command, each and every time I desire total relaxation, I am instantly and fully relaxed when I think my chosen word_____. I feel a deep sense of gratification as this word programming becomes a reality. Feeling wonderful, generous, alive, and eager to Release and Clear my negative self-image . . .

RELEASE AND CLEAR

So relaxed . . . so relaxed . . . slowly drifting into a most satisfying state of relaxation. Relaxation is good for me. I release every last ounce of useless tension . . . as I rest contentedly, to awaken when I must, refreshed and invigorated. I am alive with the feeling of freedom, of promise, of exhilarating positive expectation. My mind is clear . . . my body recharged . . . and my past deactivated . . . and left behind me.

As I relax . . . I release every unhappy experience of the past . . . and everything connected with those experiences. I find it easy to let them go. I am a part of life . . . as are we all . . . and we all move, live, and think, as we have a right to. Life goes on, and so do I . . . growing rich in experience . . . and in capacity to achieve. My positive experiences supply me with a directness to meet the challenges of my life. All I must do is use the amazing power of my subconscious mind. I am using that capacity now to disengage me from every negative . . . destructive . . . and harmful impression ever made upon me. They fade . . . fade . . . fade out of my life forever.

I am grateful and thankful for every experience of the past. I now forgive myself for every mistake I have ever made; and I forgive everyone else who may have in any way harmed me. I know that out of each experience . . . as I understand it . . . good must surely come to me. I forgive myself for every mistake because I know that each mistake is a stepping-stone to greater understanding . . . to greater opportunity . . . and to greater achievement. I grow stronger with each experience . . . and I am stronger than anything life can offer. I am preparing myself to meet its challenges directly . . . free of negative conditioning. I am more than any challenge . . . for I possess the power and the ability to channel any experience into a rich and rewarding way of life.

I now fully release the past . . . and all its effects upon me. I am free . . . free of the past . . . free to be me . . . entirely. I accept myself completely. I am a valuable and talented human being . . . I am always aware of my innate worth. There are things to be done by me . . . that are done better by me than by any other human being. Every word . . . every movement . . . every gesture of mine . . . preserves my unique stamp upon life. For as long as time has been . . . or ever shall be . . . there is no one who can exactly duplicate me. I am pleased . . . I accept myself . . . I love myself . . . I am grateful for my new level of understanding. My acceptance releases me from negative self-dislike . . . and so I am now free to change that which must be changed . . . to improve that which can be improved . . . to let go of that which is inhibiting or destructive. My self-acceptance now enables me to accept everyone else . . . I accept myself . . . I accept others as they are . . . I accept even those who are unacceptable . . . as unacceptable . . . and go on my way.

I bestow upon others my affection . . . true and unencumbered. In my imagination . . . I see them having all the good I desire for myself. What I desire for myself, I also desire for everyone else . . . I have fulfilled my nature. I have supplied myself with those priceless qualities and feelings . . . acceptance . . . love . . . and forgiveness . . . and so I now have them to give. I give them freely. I feel the warmth and excitement of building a new and rewarding life. A firm, quiet sense of self-love and self-determination dominates my every waking and sleeping hour. I am ready to release, and do so this night. CLEAR . . . CLEAR . . . CLEAR.

After you have done Release and Clear Script:

1. Remain in a relaxed state,
2. repeat your chosen alpha word, and
3. proceed to the following script for self-confidence.

SELF-CONFIDENCE

This simple act of relaxation is instruction to my deeper level of mind. To repair. To revitalize my mental thoughts to be positive and allow me to be self-confident. Now I choose to relax and let it happen. Feel safe and secure. Let go. I relax deeper and deeper. Deeper and deeper. Somewhere in my deeper awareness is my blueprint of myself as a living being. I am programming my ability to duplicate this blueprint as new cells replace the old with positive self-confidence. With guidance my mind replaces them in the positive conditioned way. In a pattern which will work well for me now and in the future.

The reason I am reading this relaxation session is that I want to release all negative emotions of anxiety and worry that relate to my self-confidence. I have made a decision to be in control of my life and my thoughts. I have decided to enjoy life and be self-confident. That's right! Great. Now I am going to do a repeat technique that will build my own internal blueprint for confidences. I am going to say the phrase with a lot of energy and excitement. I will repeat the phrase in a very special way, silently to myself, in the privacy of my own mind so I can hear the excitement as my own reality. Each time I say the phrase, I will say it with more energy and excitement because I know it is my reality and that is exciting.

"I am confident, strong and brave today and for the rest of my life."
"I am confident, strong and brave today and for the rest of my life."
"I am confident, strong and brave today and for the rest of my life."
"I am confident, strong and brave today and for the rest of my life."

I now instruct my deeper mind to replace and renew my old pattern concerning self-confidence with a new instruction to release the old pattern. To deliver to myself a new pattern following the guidelines presented here and now. I now impress my deeper awareness with a definite mental image of dynamic self-confidence. I accept myself as a lovable person with the ability to express and receive love. I am unique. I have special qualifications. There are things for me to do that are done better by me than by any other person.

I am important to life. I live in such a way that I approve of myself. I have confidence in my own judgment. I am honest and dependable. My integrity is felt by everyone I meet. Through my creative thinking I now direct my life into wholesome and complete expression. I see myself expressing radiant vitality and boundless energy. I have the power to control my thoughts and direct it toward constructive and wise decisions. I have the courage and faith in myself to act with complete confidence. Within myself is a storehouse of untapped vitality, strength and courage. I now have faith in myself as I rely on this new self-confident power.

I find abundant courage and confidence in myself. As I reach a new dimension many new doors open to me. Opportunities stimulate me to achieve much more satisfaction then I have ever experienced before. I soon recognize this dynamic change in my character and develop a new appreciation and respect for myself. I have faith and believe in myself. I am considerate and gentle to my loved ones and share me rewards generously. I am an individual who desires the finest life has to offer. My conscious thoughts inspire the way. I find my own intention for life.

I am aware of these thoughts. They are becoming increasingly positive and helpful to my well-being. My deeper mind now supplies the means of fulfilling all of my suggestions. I realize that genuine understanding and confidence in my uniqueness is a matter of gradual growth and development. As I faithfully plant the seeds of trust, of confidence in myself, my ability to express in my own unique way increases constantly. I enjoy the deep satisfaction of a now peaceful and enriching life. I now deeply impress my deeper mind with a mental image of dynamic self-confidence.

I demand of myself complete expression, earnestly and sincerely believing in myself to be strong, brave, courageous, successful and self-confident.

I realize that I now have the power to express self-confidence, so that it acts as a powerful magnet to attract success and confidence in myself. Now allowing the law of attraction to be activated and strong within me toward what I truly want. My thoughts go directly toward what I want most. I favorably influence all persons by my positive inner attitude. I project feelings of cooperation to people, and my belief in myself is evident to all around me. My attitude toward people is helpful and cooperative, and I know that this positive attitude brings me success and happiness. I know that my self-confidence is increased by thinking power-generating thoughts. I think of myself as strong, resourceful, and self-reliant. I now have an inner consciousness of myself as agreeable, graceful, and pleasant. I have a genuine interest in others, which in turn increases my self-assurance. I sincerely enjoy communicating with others. Listening, speaking with assurance. The quality of my voice expresses power, self-confidence, and caring, and I have a well-modulated tone that expresses a positive and self-controlled person. All of my actions express my confident attitude. My eyes are straightforward. My body posture reflects confidence. My manner of walking is brisk and energetic.

I accept myself as a lovable person with the ability to express and receive love. I am unique. My positive thoughts generate positive energy around me. I choose my thoughts with a positive attitude. Directing them toward all positive feelings and then listening to my feelings. I attract positive energy from all around me. I have special qualifications. There are things for me to do that are done better by me than by any other person.

I respect myself and I realize that people accept me and highly regard me. I have a high and honest opinion of myself, and I expect respect and consideration from all people. People believe in me because I now believe in myself and in my power to achieve. I continuously grow in self-confidence, courage, strength. Because I express my inner power by dynamic action, I realize a bright new life, full of personal achievement. I quietly accept the wonderful knowledge that I now express my highest ideal. I am dynamic. I believe in myself. I have dynamic self-confidence. I can and do achieve easily and effectively all that is in my best interest for my highest good.

This entire suggestion is represented by the color yellow. Yellow symbolizes strength and power to achieve my outcomes. My outcome is a self-confident me. And I now feel the strength and power flowing into my body and mind. I feel the golden yellow color filling my veins with self-confidence. And I am pleased. I continue to have unwavering faith. I keep faithfully planting the seeds of self-confidence. I secure the knowledge and my deeper awareness carries them out for me according to my instructions, my ability to express these new instructions is now increased and I enjoy the deep quiet satisfaction of a new peaceful self-confident life. Every time I see yellow, whether consciously or subconsciously, this session is doubled in my subconscious mind, allowing it to have the maximal potential in my life.

This entire suggestion is represented by the letter "D" of my sub-key word "Discover." Anytime I think, say, or see the word "Discover," all suggestions keyed to this word are automatically activated, stimulated and work for my benefit.

You now have the choice to either awaken or to drift off into a normal, natural sleep. If you are going to awaken, say:

Twenty minutes. Wide awake.

If you are going to drift off into a normal, natural sleep, say:

I am now going to drift off into a normal, natural sleep. When I awaken, I will feel fully rested, calm, and at peace with myself, the world, and those around me.

E=Evaluate Your Progress

After you have gone through the entire **DISCOVER PROCESS** once, evaluate your level of self-confidence. Do you still carry the same fears you listed at the beginning? Have you incorporated qualities of the person you modeled into your life?

_____

_____

_____

_____

_____

_____

_____

_____

_____

_____

_____

_____

_____

R=Revise & Repeat

If you have achieved your goal, congratulations! Read the following DISCOVER Flash Cards before you retire to bed each night, and repeat the word "Discover" to compound the contents of the scripts from the **DISCOVER PROCESS**.

If you haven't achieved your goal, redo the Self-Confidence Key, including all exercises, and read or listen to the script for Self-Confidence for another 21 days.

I am Confident, Strong, and Brave today.	I am important to life.
I have abundant courage and confidence in myself.	I have faith and I believe in myself.
I accept myself as a lovable person.	I appreciate my radiant vitality and boundless energy.
I know that my self-confidence is increased by thinking power-generated thoughts.	I have a high and honest opinion of myself.
I continuously grow in self-confidence, courage, and strength.	I now believe in myself and in my power to achieve.

Self-Talk

From Denigrating to Elevating

"A self that goes on changing is a self that goes on living." —*Virginia Woolf*

What goes on in your head when you talk to yourself? Are you empowering yourself? Are you insulting yourself? Are you saying things that are going to help you reach your goals? Are you sabotaging yourself? It's time to look at your self talk and transform your talk to elevating with the **DISCOVER PROCESS**.

D=Decide to Change

In the space provided, write about what you say to yourself that is not elevating. Do you focus on the past or the future, or on factors outside of your control? Do you demand perfection? What words do you regularly use that are sabotaging you (e.g., try, hope, problem, can't not, bad, must/gotta/have to, always/never/completely)? Begin with some form of the following affirmation: *I acknowledge that I am* Perfect Enough *and I recognize and embrace this opportunity to elevate my self-talk.*

_____

_____

_____

_____

_____

_____

_____

I=Identify Your Fears

What fears keep you from speaking positively about yourself, either in your own head or out loud? Write the profile for your fears, including the fear of sounding too positive or conceited. Where did your fears come from? When did they come into your life and why?

_____

_____

_____

_____

_____

_____

_____

_____

_____

_____

_____

S=Self-Inquiry

Think about what in your life generated positive thoughts and/or made you feel good which produced positive thoughts. Go ahead and give yourself credit for your positive actions. How have you successfully, positively spoken about yourself in the past?

_____

_____

_____

_____

_____

_____

_____

_____

_____

_____

_____

_____

_____

_____

_____

C=Conscious-Level Action Steps

Evaluate your self-talk. How does it need to be changed?

_____

_____

_____

_____

_____

_____

_____

_____

_____

CHANGING YOUR SELF-TALK

There are two ways to eliminate negative self-talk. One is through a process commonly referred to as *thought-stopping,* which involves four steps:

1. Become aware of self-talk.
2. Stop the negative.
3. Replace with positive.
4. Practice the act of stopping negative thoughts.

CONTROLLING YOUR INTERNAL AND EXTERNAL DIALOGUE

Cancel and *Snap it!* are methods I use to help people stop their negative thinking (i.e., stinkin' thinkin'). You are the only person who can, within a moment of thinking or saying something, stop that thought. You are at the control panel of your thinking.

CANCEL

The moment you catch yourself saying something negative, say "cancel," out loud, and replace the thought with something positive. If you have difficulty coming up with a replacement, override your negative thought or word with the image of a purple elephant. *Why?* Because there's no such thing as a purple elephant; it doesn't exist. Therefore, you couldn't have developed any kind of negative association with it. It merely takes up some space for a moment, and you move on. Cancel works well for don't, nots, and woulda/coulda/shoulda's!

SNAP IT!

In order to reinforce your *Cancel,* you can snap a rubber band on your wrist. I learned this from Bob Reese, author of *Develop the Winner's Mentality.* Snapping the rubber band biologically triggers the canceling of the negative thought; the slight pain changes the thought on a deeper level than the *Cancel* alone. Optimally, you then replace your thought with a positive one. And again, if you have difficulty coming up with one in that moment, you envision a purple elephant.

TIPS FOR IMPROVING YOUR AUTOSUGGESTIONS (I.E., YOUR LANGUAGE AND TO WRITE YOUR OWN SCRIPTS)

Here are some simple rules to follow when structuring your language—to yourself or two others. You can also use these rules when creating affirmations or suggestions when writing your own self-hypnosis script for losing weight, quitting smoking, or whatever else you'd like to accomplish. Remember that your language creates action in the world and that language (both negative and positive) programs your subconscious. And when you're in Alpha state, your language will program your subconscious very quickly, and very easily, so as they say, *"Be careful what you wish for . . . "*

1.   **Be realistic.** Though your subconscious mind doesn't recognize the concept of impossible, and will work on anything, there are five areas to avoid, particularly when you are in Alpha state.

   a.   *Avoid working on the mind of another.* The one mind you know you can control is your own. Besides, the universe doesn't reward people who try to control the minds of others.

   b.   *Avoid attempting to change the orderly progression of time.*

   c.   *Avoid thinking you can call upon knowledge, information, and experience you don't have* (e.g., you can't fly, you don't have bionic vision or hearing, and if you have no experience in running, no affirmation or suggestion will make you an instant, marathon runner).

   d.   *Avoid the attempt to make physical changes that are physically impossible* (e.g., although some nonhuman animals can re-grow limbs, we cannot. And although I have heard people tell me they used affirmations to increase their bust size, I'm a bit wary of this technique.)

   e.   *Avoid manipulation of that which is beyond your control (e.g., the weather).*

2.   **Phrase everything in the present time.** When you say, "I will," you're not really committing to do anything now. In fact, you're not really committing to do anything at all; all you're doing is saying you plan to do it . . . later. And for most people, later never comes. Create a strong mental image of your objective "NOW" and let your subconscious produce it for you.

3.   **Always use a completely non-resistant (positive) approach.** As long as you talk about what's bothering you, you give it energy; you feed and nurture it simply by paying attention to it. And that makes it more likely that it will live on and recur. Instead, make no mention of what's bothering you. Create a dynamic and positive image of your objective.

4.   **State your objective clearly**. Fuzzy, vague goals produce little in the way of results. Always work for the strongest possible response—feelings and pictures. Know exactly what you want, and state it and see it in full color and three dimensions, along with all the feelings it elicits.

5.   **Stress activity.** Stress the activity toward your objective. Visualize your active participation. Begin your activity NOW.

6.   **Visualize.** Remember that Alpha consciousness responds only to mental images. So when you're in Alpha, imagine the desired goal as you produce Alpha brainwaves. Let the image happen.

7.   **Symbolize.** Any concept, goal, or objective that doesn't lend itself easily to visualization can be readily impressed into the subconscious mind by simply assigning a symbol to it. For example, whenever anyone says "refrigerator," an image appears in your consciousness. You then have a feeling of delight, a feeling of anger, a blah feeling, a feeling of excitement—any number of responses are triggered according to your experiences. In this same manner, you can deliberately use words, colors, objects, people, or things to trigger entire affirmations and/or suggestions.

Here are some examples of helpful affirmations that my clients often use:
- I handle stress and tension appropriately and effectively.
- My mood is calm and relaxed.
- I cope well and get on with my life during times of stress.
- My breathing is deep, slow, and calm.
- I am a confident and believe in myself.

Write little reminders, goals and affirmations on note cards and place these cards where they can see them at the start of their day. If you're having trouble with your mindset, try making one that says, "I am relaxed and confident that I am achieving my ideal body weight." Repeat this phrase to yourself often and with a lot of enthusiasm. Before you know it, you'll notice an improvement and you will lose weight!

ACTION STEP
MODELING POSITIVE SELF-TALK

- Who speaks well of themselves and their life and future?

_____

- Close your eyes and imagine that person.
- Envision how the person stands, how they walk, and how they use their hands and eyes. Listen to that person speak.
- Imagine that person interacting with others. What does their voice sound like?

_____

- What kinds of things do they frequently say to describe their career and relationships?

_____

- Observe how the other people react to your person who speaks well of their life, yet isn't boastful.
- Imagine yourself standing close to the person you'd like to model. How do you feel?

_____

- Can you feel their contentment?

_____

- Pretend you're a human sponge and soak up all their good language and feelings.
- Turn to the people in your vision and watch them react to you the same way they reacted to the person you're modeling. Feel the respect and admiration from those around you.

- Now, open your eyes.

- What are your thoughts and feelings about your modeling experience?

_____

_____

_____

_____

_____

_____

_____

_____

O=Outcome Development Board

Cut out and paste photos and words that represent your model of self-talk, and words and images that represent your past success onto section#2 of your outcome board. The bulk of this particular section will probably be words, so choose them wisely. You are creating a story with your board of what you want your outcomes to be, and you will begin that story with "I am….."

Here are some tips for choosing the most effective images and words:

- Look for words that you would like to have in your everyday vocabulary
- Choose positive words only.
- Use your information from your self-inquiry.

What are your thoughts and feelings regarding your experience of completing this first section of your outcome board?

_____

_____

_____

_____

_____

_____

_____

_____

_____

_____

V=Visualize, with the Help of Hypnosis

USE HYPNOSIS TO TURBO-CHARGE YOUR NEW SELF-TALK

Everything we've done so far is on the conscious level. Now, let's turbo-charge the improvements you'd like to make regarding your self-talk by enlisting your subconscious through hypnosis! As with any self-hypnosis script, you must relax yourself first by using Instant Alpha Conditioning. You can read the positive self-talk script each time, you can record yourself, or you can listen to the Perfect Enough CD called "Positive Self-Talk." By reprogramming your subconscious mind, you automatically embed positive words and thoughts into the deeper levels of your mind and those words soon become your own positive self-talk.

Let's work with 88% of your brain, and get your every thought to be more positive!

INSTANT ALPHA CONDITIONING

Instructions:

1. Use the word you selected to replace the longer version of the Alpha conditioning technique. Read the following script and let Alpha occur each night, before retiring, for 21 nights. If you miss a night, you must begin again. Read aloud, with feeling.

2. Proceed immediately to the script for Positive Self-Talk.

S	M	T	W	Th	F	Sat

From this moment on, each and every time I desire to attain the deep state of total relaxation, I am instantly and fully relaxed, as I am now drifting into the Alpha state of consciousness. The moment I think my chosen word _____, Alpha occurs. This word has an effect only when I use it and only under the proper circumstances. Each and every time I do use it I am fully prepared to receive positive, beneficial and constructive suggestions, impressing each one deeper into my storage and memory facility of my brain.

From this moment on, _____ triggers deep relaxation of my mind and body. I feel Alpha occur. I feel wonderful. I feel comfortable. I am totally receptive and responsive to my own creative ideas and suggestions. I am bathed in a glow of quietness, peace, and serenity. My chosen word works only when I deliberately use it for deep relaxation to attain Alpha consciousness. Its use in regular conversation has no effect on me whatsoever. From this moment on, each and every time I desire the deep state of total relaxation, I am instantly and fully relaxed upon saying _____. Because my subconscious must follow my command, each and every time I desire total relaxation, I am instantly and fully relaxed when I think my chosen word_____. I feel a deep sense of gratification as this word programming becomes a reality. Feeling wonderful, generous, alive, and eager to increase my positive self-talk . . .

POSITIVE SELF-TALK

When negative thoughts enter my mind about myself, I mentally say the word "CANCEL" to myself. I replace any negative thought that I may have with a positive thought. Positive thoughts remain within the conscious portion of my mind much longer and much clearer than ever before. Without fail, without exception, without excuse, each and every time a negative thought or idea enters my mind, I mentally say the word "CANCEL" to myself. My personal life is in order, my private life is content, and my health is in perfect order. I see myself how I want to be. I am positive, happy, healthy and glad to be alive.

I know that being positive, happy, healthy and glad to be alive is called being "balanced." I am balanced. I understand that being "balanced" is when I feel that I am living every day happier. It is an unstoppable, powerful confidence that means that I am the best that I can be. I am always doing and achieving what I set my mind to do. I am thankful that through the power of positive thinking I have the ability to create positive actions. My internal positive self-talk allows me to achieve whatever outcomes I want to work toward. I know that when I practice positive self-talk, my subconscious mind allows positive thoughts to flow through to the conscious mind. It is easy for me to learn and create positive ways to think in all situations. It doesn't matter in the least what has happened in the past, because I am choosing to be positive now and in the future.

Every day in every way I am physically stronger and more fit. I am more alert, more wide-awake, and more energetic. Every day, from the moment I wake up, I remain deeply interested in whatever I am doing. When I work, play, my mind is much less preoccupied with things I cannot change and much more with things I can change and I'm about to change. I focus on my task at hand. Every day I live life with nerves that are stronger and steadier. When I am living life to the fullest, my mind is calm, clear and composed. I think clearly, I concentrate easily, my memory is sharp, and I see things in their true perspective and do not allow them to get out of proportion. Every day that I live my life I am emotionally calm and tranquil. I feel a wonderful sense of personal well-being, personal safety and security.

I am completely relaxed and tranquil. I have confidence in myself and in my ability to enjoy life, living with a positive attitude. I am optimistic, happy and confident. I stick up for myself, I stand on my own feet, and I hold my own ground. Things happen exactly as I wish for them to happen in my everyday life. I remain cheerful and optimistic.

No matter what is going on in my life, I always remain positive and free from negative self-talk. I am confident in my everyday abilities to enjoy life and "CANCEL" out any negative and harmful self-talk that I may have. I easily learn more positive words and statements to replace habits of negative thinking. I remain with a clear outlook for a wonderful and successful future. Every time I see the color red, it reminds me that I am positive and living my life with balance.

This entire suggestion is represented by the letter "I" of my sub-key word "Discover." Anytime I think, say, or see the word "Discover," all suggestions keyed to this word are automatically activated, stimulated and work for my benefit.

You now have the choice to either awaken or to drift off into a normal, natural sleep. If you are going to awaken, say:

Twenty minutes. Wide awake.

If you are going to drift off into a normal, natural sleep, say:

I am now going to drift off into a normal, natural sleep. When I awaken, I will feel fully rested, calm, and at peace with myself, the world, and those around me.

E=Evaluate Your Progress

After you have gone through the entire **DISCOVER PROCESS** once, evaluate your level of self-talk. Do you still carry the same fears you listed at the beginning? Have you incorporated qualities of the person you modeled into your life? Are you aware of being more positive? Are you talking more positively?

_____

_____

_____

_____

_____

_____

_____

_____

_____

_____

_____

_____

R=Revise & Repeat

If you have achieved your goal, congratulations! Read the following DISCOVER Flash Cards before you retire to bed each night, and repeat the word "Discover" to compound the contents of the scripts from the *DISCOVER PROCESS*.

If you haven't achieved your goal, redo the Self-Talk Key, including all exercises, and read or listen to the script for Self-Talk for another 21 days.

I am optimistic and happy.	I create positive words for my everyday thinking.
I remember the word CANCEL to let go of negative thoughts.	My internal positive self-talk allows me to achieve the outcomes I am working toward.
I am living life to the fullest.	I feel a wonderful sense of personal well-being, personal safety and security.
I am glad to be alive and balanced.	My mind is calm, clear, and composed.
I always remain positive and optimistic.	My mind is good at generating positive thoughts.

Key 3

PERSISTENCE

From Hesitation to Determination

"Think you can't or think you can… either way, you will be right!" —Henry Ford

TOP 10 OBSTACLES TO PERSISTENCE

10. IMAGINING FAILURE.

If you visualize yourself smoking again, drinking again, living paycheck-to-paycheck, or in yet another abusive or miserable relationship, guess what's going to happen?

9. ACTING NERVOUS.

When you allow yourself to act nervous, your body language, your movement, and your voice, all tell the world how vulnerable you are. Those around you will hear that message, and many people will react negatively and/or judge you as being insecure or maybe even incompetent. And nothing confirms your feelings of insecurity like the absence of confidence from those around you.

8. STRESSING ABOUT WHAT OTHER PEOPLE THINK OF YOU.

"Everyone knows I've been trying to lose weight and they're all just watching and waiting to see if I'll fail again. If I do, they'll lose all respect for me."

7. MAKING UNREASONABLE DEMANDS.

"If this relationship isn't *the one*, I'm never dating again and I'm joining a convent."

6. WORRYING ABOUT THINGS YOU HAVE NO CONTROL OVER.

"If this guy cheats on me, I don't know how I'll recover from it."

5. LACK OF FOCUS.

Have you ever said to yourself, "No matter how hard I work, I'm always afraid I won't have enough money to retire." As you know, if you're thinking about what might occur in the future, you're definitely not focusing on the present moment.

4. MAKING MISTAKES.

If you want to stop drinking and you keep socializing with people you usually get drunk with, your sobriety won't be coming any time soon.

3. THINKING YOU'RE NOT GOOD ENOUGH.

"Maybe I'm not talented enough to land such a fabulous client."

2. NEGATIVE SELF-TALK.

"I don't have the willpower to make it through the holiday party without eating at least two pieces of cake." And you'll eat at least two, I promise.

THE IMPORTANCE OF YOUR MINDSET

Many people develop problems with their mindset because they begin to **overindulge** in self-criticism and self-judgment. As we learn how to train ourselves, like all other successful people, can often be own worst critics and harshest judges.

Early in my career as a hypnotherapist, I noticed a trend with people that came to me for help with their lives. All of them were extremely talented, and most were already very successful in their lives; they seemed like people who should have been incredibly confident in their abilities. So why were they having trouble with their mindset?

I began to see that it had a lot to do with the standards they were setting for themselves.

A poor or weak mindset normally is the result of over-critiquing one's traits and/or abilities to a fault. It's a result of negative self-judgment. When highly-skilled, successful and otherwise self-confident clients came to see me, I realized that the reason they were having so much trouble with their lives was that they were judging themselves not against others in their field or against their true selves, but against the *unrealistic expectation that they had to perform perfectly in life each and every time.*

The result of this pressure was counter-productive stress and anxiety that produced negative self-talk, and a self-destructive attitude that took away from the quality of their performance in life. To overcome the problems that occur because of a poor mindset, I suggest you look at yourself from a brand new perspective. Take a step back and realize that you are in very good company. The most successful people who are at the pinnacle in their fields make mistakes all the time. And they treat them as feedback and they learn from them. You can too. Mistakes don't reflect on you as a person--the way you respond to them does.

"Mistakes are essential to progress. The willingness to learn from them is the backbone of any progress. The object is to succeed, not to count your mistakes."

- Tae Yun Kim

D=Decide to Change

Your decision with regards to persistence, is the decision to have a healthy mindset about it. You want to make friends with the idea that success with weight loss, your career, your finances, and anything else, rarely comes without hard work and sticking to what you want to achieve regardless of how difficult your circumstances may appear to be. The adage, "Good things come to those who wait," can also be phrased, "Good things come to those who don't give up." What would it mean for you to go from hesitation to determination? Begin describing your thoughts and feelings with some form of the following affirmation: *I acknowledge that I am* Perfect Enough *and I recognize and embrace this opportunity to enhance my persistence.*

_____

_____

_____

_____

_____

_____

_____

_____

_____

_____

_____

I=Identify Your Fears

What fears are preventing you from having a healthy attitude of persistence in your life? Fear of making mistakes? Fear of failure? Fear of appearing incompetent because of making mistakes? Fear of appearing incompetent because you haven't succeeded in a traditional way? Write the profile of your fears. Remember, you cannot master them if you don't know them well.

_____

_____

_____

_____

_____

_____

_____

_____

_____

_____

_____

_____

S=Self-Inquiry

Visualizing and thinking about past successes is a good way to go build confidence and remind yourself that you have persisted in the past. Use any time period that you can think of, and recall a time you succeeded because you were persistent.

_____

_____

_____

_____

_____

_____

_____

_____

_____

_____

_____

_____

C=Conscious-Level Action Steps

There are many things you can do on the conscious level to increase your persistence.

1. Focus on getting organized. If you have a hard time stopping yourself from dwelling in the past, I suggest that you try to focus on your past successes rather than mistakes. Visualizing and thinking about past successes is an excellent way to remember how you felt getting thing done. *What you think about is what you become.*

    If you allow past hesitation to consume your thoughts, you are doomed to repeat past mistakes. From time to time clients come to me because they are stuck in a pattern of not getting things done. They say that they are too lazy to get organized. And guess what keeps happening? That statement gives new life to the past and recreates it in the present.

2. When you are completely relaxed and in a highly receptive state of mind, repeat the following:

    I am grateful and thankful for every experience of the past, and for everything connected with those experiences. I find it easy to let go of my past hesitations. I forgive myself for every mistake I have ever made. Life goes on, and so do I, growing rich in experience and in the capacity to achieve. I am stronger than anything life can offer. I am motivated to be a person who gets things done.

3. Mental rehearsal. When you practice in your mind (like when you create your success through Theater of the Mind), you're doing more than simply visualizing because you're using all of your senses. The only caveat is that you must believe in what you see.

4. Embrace change. Resistance to change is a surefire way to exhaust yourself and waste your time. You must love change, desire change, and understand that life *is* change. Change is not positive or negative, it merely *is.* Your reaction to change and your relationship to change are what will determine how easy it is for you to adjust.

5. Take time each day to remind yourself of all of the progress you've made,

and be grateful for that progress. Remind yourself of all the positive experiences you've had, and of all the successes you've achieved. Tell yourself that you are brave, smart, balanced, and confident. And, most important of all, remind yourself that each mistake you've made along the way has been a learning experience that has brought you to your current level in life. When you do something well, tell yourself, out loud, "I did that well." And when you do make a mistake, make sure you look for the things you did well or correctly.

6. Be deeply committed to this process. Your Positive Mental Attitude (PMA, a key Napoleon Hill concept) will keep you poised, in a state of equilibrium, and will create an environment where commitment is effortless. When you are constantly seeing and feeling the benefits of committing yourself to attaining the highest level you are capable of, those benefits and that commitment compound. They multiply exponentially (just like negativity and misery compound the more you indulge in them—so beware).

List 10 things you are grateful for that you are doing for yourself:

_____

_____

_____

_____

_____

_____

_____

_____

ACTION STEP
MODELING PERSISTENCE

- Who enjoys persisting and learns from their mistakes, always getting better and better?

_____

- Close your eyes and imagine that person.
- Envision how the person stands, how they walk, and how they use their hands and eyes. Listen to that person speak.
- Imagine that person getting things done. What does their voice sound like? What kinds of things do they frequently say to describe their ability to be persistent? Observe how the other people react to your person who speaks well of their life, yet isn't boastful, and everything they do is done in an orderly manner.
- Imagine yourself standing close to the person you'd like to model. How do you feel? Can you feel their contentment?

_____

_____

_____

_____

- Pretend you're a human sponge and soak up all their good language and feelings.
- Turn to the people in your vision and watch them react to you the same way they reacted to the person you're modeling. Feel the respect and admiration from those around you.
- Now, open your eyes.

What are your thoughts and feelings about your modeling experience?

_____

_____

_____

_____

_____

_____

_____

_____

_____

_____

_____

_____

_____

_____

_____

O=Outcome Development Board

Cut out and paste photos and words that represent your model of persistence and words and images that represent your past success onto section #3 of your outcome board. You are creating a story with your board of what you want your outcomes to be. Your story begins with "I am . . . ". What people, images, photos, and words reflect your model of persistence and how you'd like to manifest persistence? Your outcome poster is the final step you can take, on the conscious level, to create a life of happiness and balance. Here are some tips for choosing the most effective images:

- Who represents persistence to you? Is there someone in your field who has overcome adversity and obstacles, yet persisted and achieved the kind of success you'd like to achieve?
- Is there an animal that represents persistence and success to you? Beavers, squirrels, and raccoons are all persistent. They all have a goal in mind and work at it until they reach it, despite setbacks.
- Is there a company or brand that represents persistence to you? Cut out their logo and paste it onto your outcome board.

What are your thoughts and feelings regarding your experience of completing this first section of your outcome board?

_____

_____

_____

_____

_____

_____

V=Visualize, with the Help of Hypnosis

USE HYPNOSIS TO TURBO-CHARGE YOUR NEW PERSISTENCE

As I've said, persistence is a habit. You can work at it on the conscious level by practicing it, but to make certain it "takes," you should turbo-charge your efforts at persistence with self-hypnosis. As with any self-hypnosis script, you must relax yourself first by using Instant Alpha Conditioning. Afterwards, you can read the persistence script each time, you can record yourself reading it, or you can listen to the Perfect Enough CD called "Persistence."

INSTANT ALPHA CONDITIONING

Instructions:

1. Read each night, before retiring, for 21 nights. If you miss a night, you must begin again. Read aloud, with feeling. Use the word you selected to replace the longer Alpha conditioning technique. Read the following script and let Alpha occur.

S	M	T	W	Th	F	Sat

2. Proceed immediately to the script for Persistence.

From this moment on, each and every time I desire to attain the deep state of total relaxation, I am instantly and fully relaxed, as I am now drifting into the Alpha state of consciousness. The moment I think my chosen word _____, Alpha occurs. This word has an effect only when I use it and only under the proper circumstances. Each and every time I do use it I am fully prepared to receive positive, beneficial and constructive suggestions, impressing each one deeper into my storage and memory facility of my brain.

From this moment on, _____ triggers deep relaxation of my mind and body. I feel Alpha occur. I feel wonderful. I feel comfortable. I am totally receptive and responsive to my own creative ideas and suggestions. I am bathed in a glow of quietness, peace, and serenity. My chosen word works only when I deliberately use it for deep relaxation to attain Alpha consciousness. Its use in regular conversation has no effect on me whatsoever. From this moment on, each and every time I desire the deep state of total relaxation, I am instantly and fully relaxed upon saying _____. Because my subconscious must follow my command, each and every time I desire total relaxation, I am instantly and fully relaxed when I think my chosen word_____. I feel a deep sense of gratification as this word programming becomes a reality. Feeling wonderful, generous, alive, and eager to increase my persistence . . .

PERSISTENCE

The reason I am reading to this session is that I want to let go of all negative habit patterns that keep me from being a persistent individual. I am making a decision to be in control of my life by creating the habit pattern of being persistent. I have decided to become persistent in everything I do in life. I want to be more organized, and to take be in complete control of following through. That's right! I am going to say a phrase with a lot of energy and excitement. I will repeat the phrase in a very special way, silently to myself so only I can hear it, in the privacy of my own mind. I can hear the excitement as my own reality. Each time I say the phrase, I feel the energy and excitement because I know it is my reality and that is exciting.

> "I am persistent and confident in everything I do in life -
> now and for the rest of my life."
> "I am persistent and confident in everything I do in life -
> now and for the rest of my life."
> "I am persistent and confident in everything I do in life -
> now and for the rest of my life."
> "I am persistent and confident in everything I do in life -
> now and for the rest of my life."

As I follow the release and clear instructions on this session, I allow my subconscious mind to let go of all past habit patterns that are not consistent with being persistent. So now, I see myself at the beach. I am getting a mental image, like watching a movie on my own private theater in the privacy of my own mind. I see the ocean – I see the sand - I can feel a gentle breeze. As I visualize this, I make it as real as possible. I see it all in my imagination. And now very, very vividly, I allow myself to fantasize digging a deep hole in the sand. I dig the hole deeper and deeper. Now the hole is big enough and deep enough, I bury all past negative habit patterns relating to not getting things done. I am throwing all cluttering habit patterns in it. Now, as I do this I take each negative thought I have about myself— whether it's about my organizational skills, my lack of anything, and anything negative I feel about myself, and I bury each one. So now as I imagine –I make this real. I perceive every detail of this movie in my mind. I am playing the role. I am playing the part and now as I experience burying each fear in my mind. I am putting all negative thoughts about my abilities to get things done in this hole. I notice I can imagine the smell of the sand and the sea. I feel the breeze, and now I have just allowed this become my own reality. Now as I imagine throwing the sand over the hole, I close the hole—leaving everything in it that I put in it. I have thrown away all the negativity and the negative self-talk. I have thrown away all the negative-based thoughts. I am now open to new suggestions that I will accept and act upon. I am now open to all the warmth, joy and fulfillment that life has to offer. I feel glad to be alive and enthusiastic about my future. I am now calm and relaxed and a sense of peace permeates my body and mind.

I am filling my powerful subconscious mind with a vital awareness of following through with all projects and plans. From now on, persistence is one of my strong points. It is a definite asset. It is a powerful force in my personality. I am always persistent when I have a goal to accomplish. I achieve all of my outcomes. I follow through to see that all my plans and goals become reality - for I realize that there are no permanent obstacles.

There are only temporary obstacles that I can always ultimately overcome. I do this by keeping my mind and thoughts fixed firmly on my outcomes, ensuring that I constantly move towards them. Whenever I launch new projects, whenever I make bold new plans, whenever I use my intuitiveness to set fresh goals and objectives, I always follow through. I am creating them as outcomes, persistent about everything that I do. I always follow through. I always follow through. I always follow through. I bring things to completion. I use my positive thoughts to create the power of my intention to be persistent.

Persistence is a powerful force in my personality. I always follow through, even in little things. I am a person who brings things to completion. If there are projects around the house that are undone, I give them my full attention, thereby ensuring their successful completion. If there are activities in my business that need some attention, or some follow through in order to be completed, I do so. I follow through. I see to it that in all areas of my life, I leave nothing undone. My philosophy is one of following through and getting the task completed.

Following my suggestion helps and guides me to go deeper and more and more relaxed. I have a powerful force in my personality. I am always persistent when I have an outcome to accomplish. I achieve these goals in an assured, calm, relaxed way. This builds a lifetime habit pattern of success and I find that I follow through in all my activities with ease and with pleasure. It becomes easy for me, because each time that I do a good job of following through, it is easier to follow through with future activities.

I know it's important that I am confident in my ability to accomplish whatever I set my mind to. I am persistent in finishing any task I begin. My confidence builds in my own ability to do anything I put my mind to. I realize that the mighty dynamo within me, my subconscious mind, is constantly working for me.

I am building into my life this most desirable pattern of following through, of persistence, a stick-to-it-iveness and of always getting the task completed. For by doing this, I am taking giant strides towards achieving all my goals of having a powerful personality.

This ensures genuine success and satisfaction in all phases of my life. I find myself enjoying the satisfaction of a well-organized life. I relax completely as I fill my powerful subconscious mind with the awareness of my goals. I am relaxed and receptive.

I always find a way to figure out what I need to do to get any job done. I am committed to being persistent. I grow stronger every day and with every day that passes. I have wonderful outcomes for every project I plan and implement. I have a very powerful personality. I grow and move forward in life with a real purpose, being and becoming the person I intend to be. I am energized and excited about life and everything it has to offer. I use my powerful ability to stay on task and complete projects to succeed at whatever I do.

Through my magnet within I have a powerful force in my personality. My habit pattern in life is to always persistent when I have a goal to accomplish. I achieve my goals in an assured, calm, relaxed way. This builds a lifetime habit pattern of success and I find that this happens automatically as I become the best me I can be with ease and with pleasure. It becomes easy for me because each time I do a good job of following through, it is easier to follow through with future activities.

Every time I read this session, I grow more confident and self-assured in every way. And each time I attempt to achieve this wonderful sense of relaxation, I find I do it quicker and easier than the previous time. Each time I do it quicker and quicker. Each time, allowing myself to go much deeper relaxed, much quicker, and enjoying it more and more. Every time I allow my body to relax, the better I feel. And the better I feel, the more my body relaxes. With marvelous, wonderful, good feelings going through my body and, happy, contented thoughts going through my mind. Be still and feel good.

This entire suggestion is represented by the letter "S" of my sub-key word "Discover." Anytime I think, say, or see the word "Discover", all suggestions keyed to this word are automatically activated, stimulated and work for my benefit.

You now have the choice to either awaken or to drift off into a normal, natural sleep. If you are going to awaken, say:

Twenty minutes. Wide awake.

If you are going to drift off into a normal, natural sleep, say:

I am now going to drift off into a normal, natural sleep. When I awaken, I will feel fully rested, calm, and at peace with myself, the world, and those around me.

E=Evaluate Your Progress

After you have gone through the entire ***DISCOVER PROCESS*** once, evaluate your level of persistence and determination. Do you still carry the same fears you listed at the beginning? Have you incorporated qualities of the person you modeled into your life?

_____

_____

_____

_____

_____

_____

_____

_____

_____

_____

_____

_____

_____

_____

R=Revise & Repeat

If you have achieved your goal, congratulations! Use the following DISCOVER Flash Cards before you retire to bed each night to reinforce your positive progress.

If you haven't achieved your goal, redo the Persistence Key, including all exercises, and read or listen to the script for Persistence for another 21 days.

I am persistent and confident in every thing I do in life	I follow through with all projects and plans.
I constantly move towards getting projects completed.	Persistence is a powerful force in my personality.
I bring things to completion.	I give projects my full attention insuring their successful completion.
I leave nothing undone.	I realize that the mighty dynamo within me, my subconscious mind, is constantly working for me.
I always find a way to figure out what I need to do to get any job done.	I am more confident and self assured in every way.

LIFE AND ALIVENESS

FROM LIFELESSNESS TO VITALITY

"Believe that life is worth living and your belief will help create the fact."
—*William James*

*Are you growing and developing into the person you were meant to be? Do you live your life with gusto, savoring every moment? If not, it's time to transform that lifelessness into vitality using the **DISCOVER PROCESS**.*

D=Decide to Change

If you don't have the vitality that is necessary to achieve balance and happiness, your first step is to decide that you'd like to develop that vitality. In this space provided, write about your decision to increase your vitality. Begin with some form of the following affirmation: *I acknowledge that I am* Perfect Enough *and I recognize and embrace this opportunity to enhance my vitality.*

_____

_____

_____

_____

_____

_____

_____

_____

_____

I=Identify Your Fears

What fears are keeping you from the passion for life that you crave? List your fears and write their biographies.

_____

_____

_____

_____

_____

_____

_____

_____

_____

_____

_____

_____

_____

S=Self-Inquiry

Visualizing and thinking about past positive experiences is an excellent way to build confidence and self-esteem. What you think about is what you become. Therefore, when you concentrate on your past positive experiences, you help to create future ones. Examine your life and recall a time (or times) when you exhibited passion, vitality, and aliveness. You can even use a time from your childhood, as many people lose their vitality as they age. When were you thrilled to be alive and living?

_____

_____

_____

_____

_____

_____

_____

_____

_____

_____

_____

_____

C=Conscious Level Action Steps

1. *Realize you control your own happiness.* With each moment you can choose what kind of person you'd like to be. You can decide that you'll learn the lessons you've been given in the past, and proceed as a wiser, more balanced individual. If you pause and think before you speak--if you choose your words with intent and focus on choosing only positive words--your happiness will increase.

2. *Choose peak experiences.* Whether you're planting orchids or biking through the mountains, you increase your vitality when you honor the gift of life by approaching what you're doing with zest. Celebrate all of the things your wonderful body and mind are capable of, rather taking them for granted.

3. *Be prepared.* No amount of hypnosis is going to help you if you aren't prepared to do your best.

4. *Imagine peak performance.* Imagine yourself giving the optimal performance. Create a complete, rich sensory experience. Imagine what you look like, how you feel, what you smell, and what you hear. The more detailed your image is, the better.

5. *Control your environment.* You can't control everything, but you can control who you spend time with and how you react to them. If there is someone in your life who "pushes all of your buttons," either don't spend time with that person, or change the way you react to them and their behavior.

ACTION STEP
MODELING LIFE AND ALIVENESS

- Who represents life and aliveness to you? Who chooses to be happy rather than allow obstacles to alter their mood or outlook?

_____

- Close your eyes and imagine that person.
- Envision how the person stands, how they walk, and how they use their hands and eyes.
- Imagine that person interacting with others. What does their voice sound like? What do they look like when they're listening? Observe how the other people react to your confident person.
- Imagine yourself standing close to your person who has chosen happiness. How do you feel? Can you feel their vitality?
- Pretend you're a human sponge and soak up the happiness and vitality of your model.
- Turn to the people in your vision and watch them react to you the same way they reacted to your happy person. Feel their respect and admiration, and feel your happiness and vitality.
- Now, open your eyes.

What are your thoughts and feelings about your modeling experience?

_____

_____

_____

_____

_____

_____

_____

_____

_____

_____

_____

O=Outcome Development Board

Cut out and paste photos and words that represent your model of vitality and words and images that represent your past experiences of passion and aliveness onto section #4 of your outcome board. You are creating a story with your board of what you want your outcomes to be, and your story begins with "I am . . . ". Here are some tips for choosing the most effective images:

- Use your information from your self-inquiry to find images that represent the positive experience(s) from your past.
- Think back to your modeling exercise and how you have defined the kind of vitality you'd like to have. For some people, vitality means action, while for others it means serenity and stillness. Think about that as you choose your images.
- Unless you know the intimate details of someone's life, it is difficult to say for certain that they are happy. But you will recognize outer signs of happiness, and certainly outer signs of vitality, when you see them. Choose images that *represent* the feeling you want to have and exude.
- Look for images of the body you would like to have, but keep it realistic for your height and body type.
- Look for pictures of people with the facial expressions and posture similar to the person you modeled in the modeling Action Step above.

What are your thoughts and feelings regarding your experience of completing this first section of your outcome board?

_____

_____

_____

_____

_____

_____

_____

_____

_____

_____

_____

_____

_____

_____

_____

_____

V=Visualize, with the Help of Hypnosis

USE HYPNOSIS TO TURBO-CHARGE YOUR NEW LIFE AND ALIVENESS

After you've done whatever you can on the conscious level to prepare yourself for living life to the fullest *and enjoying it*, you can reinforce your love of life and your confidence in yourself of the subconscious level. Let's open you to deeper levels of awareness of life and your role in it, along with a true knowledge that you are all that you aspire to be. Let's retrain your brain toward life and aliveness! As always, we begin with jetting you into a receptive state by way of Instant Alpha Conditioning. After that, you can either read the life and aliveness script each time, record yourself reading it and listen to it, or listen to the Perfect Enough CD called "Life and Aliveness."

Let's kick start your vitality and your enthusiasm for life by retraining your subconscious mind!

INSTANT ALPHA CONDITIONING

Instructions:

1. Read Instant Alpha each night, before retiring, for 21 nights. If you miss a night, you must begin again. Read aloud, with feeling, using the word you chose earlier to replace the longer version of Alpha conditioning.
2. Proceed immediately to the script for Life and Aliveness.

S	M	T	W	Th	F	Sat

From this moment on, each and every time I desire to attain the deep state of total relaxation, I am instantly and fully relaxed, as I am now drifting into the Alpha state of consciousness. The moment I think my chosen word, _____, Alpha occurs. This word has an effect only when I use it and only under the proper circumstances. Each and every time I do use it I am fully prepared to receive positive, beneficial and constructive suggestions, impressing each one deeper into my storage and memory facility of my brain.

From this moment on, _____ triggers deep relaxation of my mind and body. I feel Alpha occur. I feel wonderful. I feel comfortable. I am totally receptive and responsive to my own creative ideas and suggestions. I am bathed in a glow of quietness, peace, and serenity. My chosen word works only when I deliberately use it for deep relaxation to attain Alpha consciousness. Its use in regular conversation has no effect on me whatsoever. From this moment on, each and every time I desire the deep state of total relaxation, I am instantly and fully relaxed upon saying _____. Because my subconscious must follow my command, each and every time I desire total relaxation, I am instantly and fully relaxed when I think my chosen word_____. I feel a deep sense of gratification as this word programming becomes a reality. Feeling wonderful, generous, alive, and eager to live . . .

LIFE AND ALIVENESS

I continue to instruct my deeper mind to let go completely. Deeper and deeper and deeper. I am a flexible and enthusiastic human being. Life is an exciting adventure. Each day I become aware, more and more aware of the beauty and goodness of people. I like people.

From the alive and loving part of nature, I am filled with energy and enthusiasm. I make friends easily for the confidence of energy flows out into the world from the serene self within. I am confident and serene. I am glad I am alive. I live the life I want to live. From a firm base of love, and enjoy every moment. A new serenity engulfs my being. As the serenity grows within me, I feel the life's enthusiastic loving and take a new step into even deeper levels of awareness of life yet to be recognized. I am preparing myself now to recognize the deeper levels of awareness, and to feel confident in the capacity that I can know and express deeper levels of knowledge and wisdom.

Hidden within the words I repeat to myself now is the foundation for growth into higher areas of knowing. My mind intuitively knows the meaning behind the words, and gently allows the growth to take place within me. Allowing my faith to be strong and guide me to live my life with the power of intention toward my purpose. The responsibility of producing and delivering this wisdom out into the world gives me the ability to activate my own power of intention. This power gives me life and aliveness.

My feelings let me know I am alive. I am able to express my feelings. I trust my feelings and act on them. I am able to be me, expressing myself with confidence, feeling and trust. Having aliveness is being aware and being in touch with myself. Being alive, each moment, I am personally empowered.

I am flexible and enthusiastic. Life is an exciting adventure. Each day I become aware of the beauty and goodness of people. I like people and people like me. I am filled with energy and enthusiasm. I make friends easily. I am confident and serene. I appreciate myself. I live the life I want to live, and enjoy each and every moment of it.

Receiving life's energy from everything around me, the more energized I receive the more energy I give out. I bring to this moment a new image of myself that refreshes every thought about myself. I now stand tall and confident of the power within myself. I see myself superbly fulfilling every moment of my life, knowing that I am all that I aspire to be.

Once again I know that in my deeper level of awareness I know the meaning behind the words and bring to this moment a new image of myself that refreshes every thought about myself. I now stand mentally tall, confident of the power within me. I see myself superbly fulfilling every moment with grace, with wisdom. Knowing that the energy behind the words is reflected in my growth and in my interaction with life. Within me is intuitive wisdom. I trust and believe that the laws of the universe will allow me to live life to the fullest resulting in a far greater, healthier me better than I ever imagined.

I now have the flexibility, the strength, the drive, and the confidence to move forward to assume the responsibility of being the person I am meant to become, with enthusiasm, with purpose, with gentleness. I feel a wave of excitement washing over my entire being and I feel a wave of serenity behind it. I know the satisfaction of growth. A new serenity engulfs me now and I am confident, certain, and fully at ease. The beacon symbolizes this growth pattern, a light moving in a circle. The circle of love. A light brightening the path for others. A light leading the way. I see this beacon now in my imagination.

I now superimpose my love over that light and know that it reflects out into the world the energy given freely from deep within my love given unconditionally. The beacon is circling now around and around, and I move quickly and serenely into deeper levels of consciousness. Deeper than ever before. Confident and serene in the knowledge that I am safe, that I can handle the love, the flexibility, the preparation I am now enjoying. For I intuitively know I am preparing myself in ways I have yet to acknowledge, to reveal wisdom's deeper levels. This allows me to be serene. I know security and I feel secure. And when the time is right, I express with confidence, enthusiasm, and love.

I feel the warmth permeating from the beacon as it circles now round, and round and round. Deeper and higher. Deeper and higher. So high, I can see with ease. So easy higher and higher. Serene. Calm. Assurance of even greater strength flowing into my awareness. Strength to be, strength to share, strength and wisdom. Wisdom and strength reflected in the energy in which I am now a part. Slowly and with supreme confidence bring back with me what I can. And know that the rest is at this space. Whenever I visualize a beacon in my mind's eye, this space is accessible to me to feel like life's energy is flowing through me. I visualize the beacon and this space is accessible to me. Preparing me in ways beyond my current knowing to accept and then I give out with love and compassion all that I am learning. With an attitude of gratitude about what I want, I am able to allow the power of my intention to become more apparent.

All that I am experiencing is from the love center within my being. Growth and serenity. Growth and strength. Growth and wisdom. Each time I visualize the beacon, circling the light moving in a circle. The circle of love. A light brightening the path for others. A light leading the way. I am that light. I am that light. I am that light.

This entire suggestion is represented by the letter "C" of my sub-key word

"Discover." Anytime I think, say, or see the word "Discover," all suggestions keyed to this word are automatically activated, stimulated and work for my benefit.

You now have the choice to either awaken or to drift off into a normal, natural sleep. If you are going to awaken, say:

Twenty minutes. Wide awake.

If you are going to drift off into a normal, natural sleep, say:

I am now going to drift off into a normal, natural sleep. When I awaken, I will feel fully rested, calm, and at peace with myself, the world, and those around me.

E=Evaluate Your Progress

After you have gone through the entire **DISCOVER PROCESS** once, evaluate your level of aliveness, vitality, and passion for life. Do you still carry the same fears you listed at the beginning? Have you incorporated qualities of the person you modeled into your life?

_____

_____

_____

_____

_____

_____

_____

_____

_____

_____

_____

_____

_____

_____

R=Revise & Repeat

If you have achieved your goal, congratulations! Use the following DISCOVER Flash Cards before you retire to bed each night to reinforce your progress and repeat the word DISCOVER to compound the contents of the scripts.

If you haven't achieved your goal, redo the Life and Aliveness Key, including all exercises, and read or listen to the script for Life and Aliveness for another 21 days.

I am filled with energy and enthusiasm	I am glad I am alive.
Allowing my faith to be strong and guide me to live my life with the power of intention toward my purpose.	My feelings let me know I am alive.
I am flexible and enthusiastic.	I make friends easily.
I appreciate myself.	I live the life I want to live, and enjoy each and every moment of it.
I see myself superbly fulfilling every moment of my life...knowing that I am all that I aspire to be.	I trust and believe that the laws of the universe will allow me to live life to the fullest with a far greater, healthier me better than I ever imagined.

KEY 5

HEALTH

FROM ILLNESS TO WELLNESS

"The first secret you should know about perfect health is that you have to choose it. You can only be as healthy as you think it is possible to be." —Deepak Chopra

If you wouldn't describe your health as "stellar," "fantastic," or "marvelous," there is something keeping you from being healthy. And your first step toward overcoming that obstacle, resolving the issue, and achieving optimal health, is . . .

D=Decide to Change

Until you've decided that it's time you change the status of your health--and unless you believe that choice and act each day with conviction that your health is improving each day--you are likely to remain at the same weight, plagued by the same issues that are in your life (and your body and mind) today. In this space provided, write about your decision to change the status of your health. Begin with some form of the following affirmation: *I acknowledge that I am Perfect Enough and I recognize and embrace this opportunity to enhance my health.*

_____

_____

_____

_____

_____

_____

_____

_____

_____

_____

I=Identify Your Fears

What fears are keeping you from achieving optimal health? List them and write their profiles. Remember, you cannot master something if you don't know it well.

_____

_____

_____

_____

_____

_____

_____

_____

S=Self-Inquiry

Visualizing and thinking about past successes is an excellent way to build confidence and self-esteem. What you think about is what you become. Therefore, when you concentrate on your successes, you help to create future successes. *What are some of your successes regarding your health?* Can you recall a time when your health was very good and you felt fabulous and looked great? Even if you have to go back to young adulthood, describe what it's like to recall being healthy, and congratulate yourself for being healthy during that time.

_____

_____

_____

_____

_____

_____

_____

_____

_____

_____

_____

_____

C=Conscious-Level Action Steps

Fortunately, your health is one area where there are many things you can do on the conscious level to put you on a path to wellness.

1. Decrease your stress level. When your stress level increases your immunity decreases and you become more susceptible to germs, viruses, and disease. Stress leads to disease. Sometimes it's in the form of a headache, sometimes it's more serious and takes the form of an ulcer, and sometimes the result is cancer.

2. Practice relaxation as a method of stress reduction.

3. Exercise as a method of stress reduction.

4. Visualize positive images about your health. If there are any areas of your body that are currently not healthy, visualize them as healed. In fact, visualize them *healing* themselves.

5. Visualize general healing by imagining yourself as surrounded by white, shining light, like that of the healing Sun. Feel the warmth of the light circulate throughout your body and over your skin. Feel the healing as it occurs.

6. Forgive yourself. When you're judging yourself and concluding that you aren't good enough, at that moment, you're living in the past. You're focusing on one moment or series of moments from your past--whether it all happened yesterday or it's been building for your entire life--and allowing that to rule your thoughts. When you judge yourself and condemn yourself for . . . whatever . . . you're allowing your past to rule your life.

7. Forgive others. Often illness is a result of not forgiving others for the wrongs you perceive they have done to you. Release your attachment to all of the pain that others have caused you, and you'll find that your health will improve.

8. And of course, good nutrition, exercise, interruption-free sleep, meaningful work (whether or not you get paid), and intentional, wakeful relaxation of the body and mind (such as through meditation or prayer) are all components of the optimal environment for health and balance.

ACTION STEP
MODELING HEALTH

- Who is a model of health for you?

_____

- Close your eyes and imagine that person.
- Envision how the person stands, how they walk, and how they use their hands and eyes. Imagine how great they look in their clothes. Imagine the bright whites of their eyes and their clear, dewy skin.
- Imagine the daily habits of your healthy person: what they eat, how they sleep, and how they exercise. Step into the body of your healthy person while they're doing healthy things. How do you feel?

_____

_____

_____

_____

_____

- Imagine that person interacting with others. What does their voice sound like?
- Imagine yourself standing close to your healthy person. How do you feel? Can you feel their health and vitality?
- Pretend you're a human sponge and soak up the health of your model.
- Turn to the people in your vision and watch them react to you the same way they reacted to your healthy, fit person. Feel their respect and admiration, and feel your good health. Notice how your body feels alive.
- Now, open your eyes.

What are your thoughts and feelings about your modeling experience?

_____

_____

_____

_____

_____

_____

O=Outcome Development Board

Cut out and paste photos and words that represent your model of health and words and images that represent your past success in section #5 of your outcome board. You are creating a story with your board of what you want your outcomes to be, and that story begins with "I am . . . ". Here are some tips for choosing the most effective images:

- Look for images of the body you would like to have, but keep it realistic for your height and body type.
- Be careful of choosing people who look either way too thin, or way too muscular, if you're not willing to put in the time necessary to get that muscular.
- Choose someone doing activities you want to do, such as going to a spa, meditating, or practicing yoga.

What are your thoughts and feelings regarding your experience of completing this first section of your outcome board?

_____

_____

_____

_____

_____

_____

_____

_____

_____

_____

V=Visualize, with the Help of Hypnosis

USE HYPNOSIS TO TURBO-CHARGE YOUR HEALTH

After you've done what you can on the conscious level, you can program your subconscious to help you attain and maintain good health. Using hypnosis, you can turbo-charge your subconscious to promote a healthier you. As always, you must relax by using Instant Alpha Conditioning prior to reading the self-hypnosis script or listening to your recorded version. A simple way to achieve this step is to listen to the Perfect Enough CD called "Health".

Let's tap into your deeper mind to access your self-healing abilities!

INSTANT ALPHA CONDITIONING

Instructions:

1. Read each night, before retiring, for 21 nights. If you miss a night, you must begin again. Read aloud, with feeling. Use the word you selected to replace the longer version of the Alpha conditioning technique. Read the following script and let Alpha occur.

2. Proceed immediately to the script for Health or to the *Perfect Enough* CD called "Health."

S	M	T	W	Th	F	Sat

From this moment on, each and every time I desire to attain the deep state of total relaxation, I am instantly and fully relaxed, as I am now drifting into the Alpha state of consciousness. The moment I think my chosen word _____, Alpha occurs. This word has an effect only when I use it and only under the proper circumstances. Each and every time I do use it I am fully prepared to receive positive, beneficial and constructive suggestions, impressing each one deeper into my storage and memory facility of my brain.

From this moment on, _____ triggers deep relaxation of my mind and body. I feel Alpha occur. I feel wonderful. I feel comfortable. I am totally receptive and responsive to my own creative ideas and suggestions. I am bathed in a glow of quietness, peace, and serenity. My chosen word works only when I deliberately use it for deep relaxation to attain Alpha consciousness. Its use in regular conversation has no effect on me whatsoever. From this moment on, each and every time I desire the deep state of total relaxation, I am instantly and fully relaxed upon saying _____. Because my subconscious must follow my command, each and every time I desire total relaxation, I am instantly and fully relaxed when I think my chosen word_____. I feel a deep sense of gratification as this word programming becomes a reality. Feeling wonderful, generous, alive, and eager to live a healthy life . . .

HEALTH

The reason I am reading this session is because I want to improve my health. I have made a decision to be in control of my life. I have decided to enjoy radiant health. That's right! Great, now I am going to do an exercise that I believe I will really enjoy. In a moment I am going to say a phrase to myself and then I will repeat that phrase with a lot of energy and excitement. I will repeat the phrase in a very special way, silently to myself so only I, in the privacy of my own mind, can hear the excitement as my reality. Each time I say the phrase, I repeat it with more energy and excitement because I know it is my reality and that is exciting. After I say the phrase a few times I will find I believe it and own it to be true for myself.

I am strong, balanced and healthy now and for the rest of my life.
I am strong, balanced and healthy now and for the rest of my life.
I am strong, balanced and healthy now and for the rest of my life.
I am strong, balanced and healthy now and for the rest of my life.
I am strong, balanced and healthy now and for the rest of my life.
I am strong, balanced and healthy now and for the rest of my life.
I am strong, balanced and healthy now and for the rest of my life.

In my imagination I see myself going across a field to a meadow. I allow my mind to visualize, see or imagine a meadow. I look at all the details. I imagine a gentle breeze blowing. I see the waves as they flow over the grass. I feel the gentle breeze flow through my hair. Breathing in and out and relaxing even more. Deeply and completely as I enjoy this walk. The path that I am following is by a stream. I listen to the sounds of nature. Listen to the bubbling water. Listen to the rustling leaves. I put my hand into the water and notice the crisp coolness. I continue to walk on.

There is a mountain a short distance from me. As I approach the mountain I know deep within that it is easy for me to climb it. Step by step, I climb the mountain. A feeling of complete comfort flows over my body and relaxation allows me to feel comfortable safe and secure.

I face the sun as it rises like a ball of fire in the heavens. The sun is a source of energy and life. It is the source of expanding rays. I let the sun's rays bathe my body.

I let its radiance penetrate deeply into my being. I feel life-giving, healing properties flowing through my body. The sun's tremendous energies flow throughout my entire being, invigorating and strengthening every particle. It doesn't matter in the least what I have experienced in the past. Radiant health is mine right now. I feel it pulsing through me with every breath I take. Every gland, every organ, every tissue in my body is now being charged with radiant vitality, with energy. The power of my subconscious mind keeps my lungs breathing, my heart beating, my blood circulating and every gland and organ operating completely. I know it. I trust it. I believe it. I thank it for serving me so intelligently and so efficiently. At this moment, every part of my body is being cleansed, purified, revitalized.

I am strong, I am well, and I am balanced. I know that there is nothing impossible for my creative mind. Its healing power strengthens and perfects my body right now. I accept it and relax completely. I allow this energy to operate fully and freely. I let my body and mind completely relax. Life circulates normally and naturally through every tissue of my body. Every cell is alive and tingling with dynamic health. I am building new cells to replace damaged ones. Making rough ones, smooth. Every cell is alive and tingling with dynamic health.

Abundant life now operates through my eyes. I can see the beauty of life without effort. My vision is excellent. I see clearly. I hear easily. My hearing is keen and clear. Every gland and organ of my body functions in harmony. I love my body. I have faith in it. I trust it. Every part of it. I think only good thoughts about my body. I relax and handle every situation that life has to offer. I attract to me that is good for my health.

Every fiber, every tissue, every organ, every gland, every part of my body will triple in relaxation when I close my eyes. I feel great, I feel wonderful, I feel fine, with marvelous feelings going through my body and very happy, content thoughts going through my mind. Once my eyes are closed I keep relaxing with every breath I breathe. I give in to the relaxation easily and automatically, and will let myself go, relaxing more and more every time I read this session. I let myself go and all tension leaves my body. All discomfort leaves my body. All of my organs function normally, and all of my glands function normally.

I speak with love and with understanding in a completely relaxed way. I do whatever I should do. Whatever I need to do easily and confidently. I am always conscious of creative power expressing through me. I allow the feeling of relaxation to flow through my body quietly and peacefully. Knowing that this creative power with its abundant goodness continuously operates through my thoughts. Through my body and out into my world. I am confident, I am relaxed, and I am at peace. My body is being renewed and strengthened as I relax and allow the sun's rays to bathe my body. I let its radiance penetrate deeply into my being.

I allow the feeling of life-giving, healing properties to descend into my body. It's easy for me to believe in the new positive thoughts about life that I am now incorporating into my everyday thoughts. I let these feelings remain with me. And with every breath I take I continue to relax deeper, deeper, deeper.

As I count from **FIVE** down to **ONE** each one of the suggestions make positive changes through my own thoughts to let my body do what is necessary to be healthy. Allow the feeling of a cool breeze to flow across my skin. Allow the bright sunlight to heal.

FIVE…. Radiant health is pulsing through me with every breath that I take. **FOUR**… Every gland every organ and every tissue of my body is now being charged with radiant vitality and energy.

Number **THREE**… Every gland and organ is operating in harmony. Every part of me is being cleansed, purified, revitalized.

Number **TWO**… There is nothing impossible for my creative mind. This healing power strengthens and perfects my body right now. I accept it. I allow this energy to operate fully and freely. Life is circulating normally and naturally through every tissue of my body. Every cell is alive and tingling with dynamic health. Whatever my mind can conceive my mind can achieve.

ONE… I accept I can love my body. I allow myself to have faith in it. I trust every part of it. I speak with love and with understanding in a completely relaxed way. Easily and competently, and always conscious of creative power expressing through me. Once I close my eyes I will relax quietly and peacefully, knowing that this creative power with its abundant goodness continuously operates through my thoughts, through my body, and out into my world. I am confident, I am at peace.

Once I close my eyes all sounds will fade and all I notice is the sound of the brook. The bubbling water as it winds its way down the mountain. I will begin my descent down from the mountain along the brook, returning to the meadow. And as I return, I find myself eager to sit under a tree. As I sit under the tree, I know that it doesn't matter in the least what I have experienced in the past. Radiant health is mine right now. I feel it pulsing through me with every breath that I inhale. Every gland, every organ, every tissue of my body is now being charged with radiant vitality with energy.

The power of my subconscious mind keeps every gland and organ operating in harmony. My body is finding the balanced place it knows. I know it. I trust it. I thank it for serving me so intelligently and so efficiently. I also realize that at this very moment every part of me is being cleansed, purified by the light. I know that there is nothing impossible for my subconscious mind. Its healing power strengthens and perfects my body right now. I accept it and relax completely. I let this energy operate fully and freely. As I relax deeper and deeper, life's circulates normally and naturally through every tissue of my body. Every cell is alive.

I am allowing the building of new cells to replace damaged ones, making rough ones smooth. Every cell is alive and tingling with dynamic health. I am grateful for my health. Abundant life now operates through me. I love my body. I trust every part of it. I do whatever is necessary easily and confidently. I allow my creative subconscious mind to express through me, knowing that this creative power with its abundant goodness continuously operates through my thoughts, through my body, and through my mind. I am at peace.

As I sit or lie here more comfortable with each second, more relaxed, I imagine in my mind the color blue. For me, blue represents health. Every time I see or even think of the color blue I feel healthy. Blue makes me feel great about myself. The blue of the sky, a blue stripe on shirt, or even a mental image of the color blue.

Blue in any form, real or imagined, is my key to dynamic health. Any time I see the color blue, in and out of my conscious awareness, it automatically doubles this entire session for health in my subconscious mind.

My body is balanced, renewed and strengthened.

Every time I read this session I automatically go deeper relaxed and I automatically double this session in my subconscious mind.

This entire suggestion is represented by the letter "O" of my sub-key word "Discover." Anytime I think, say, or see the word "Discover," all suggestions keyed to this word are automatically activated, stimulated and work for my benefit.

You now have the choice to either awaken or to drift off into a normal, natural sleep. If you are going to awaken, say:
Twenty minutes. Wide awake.
If you are going to drift off into a normal, natural sleep, say:
I am now going to drift off into a normal, natural sleep. When I awaken, I will feel fully rested, calm, and at peace with myself, the world, and those around me.

E=Evaluate Your Progress

After you have gone through the entire **DISCOVER PROCESS** once, evaluate your level of health and wellness. Do you still carry the same fears you listed at the beginning? Have you incorporated qualities of the person you modeled into your life?

_____

_____

_____

_____

_____

_____

_____

_____

_____

_____

_____

_____

_____

_____

_____

R=Revise & Repeat

If you have achieved your goal, congratulations! Read the following DISCOVER Flash Cards before you retire to bed each night, and repeat the word "Discover" to compound the contents of the scripts from the *DISCOVER PROCESS*.

If you haven't achieved your goal, redo the Health Key, including all exercises, and read or listen to the script for Health for another 21 days.

I am at peace.	I love my body. I trust every part of it.
Its healing power strengthens and perfects my body right now.	Radiant health is mine right now.
I am strong, balanced and healthy now.	I am strong, I am well, and I am balanced.
I can see the beauty of life without effort.	I love my body. I have faith in it. I trust it.
I allow the feeling of relaxation to flow through my body quietly and peacefully.	I speak with love and with understanding in a completely relaxed way.

KEY 6

LOVE

FROM WORTHLESS TO VALUABLE

*"Everything that irritates us about others can lead us to
an understanding of ourselves."* —Carl Jung

The love you want and deserve is waiting for you. But for most people, it takes some work to attract it and maintain it. You can begin inviting love into your life with the **DISCOVER PROCESS**.

D=Decide You Want and Deserve Love

Have you made a conscious decision to attract love? Have you told the universe that you want and deserve love, and that you'll treasure it and treat it well? If not, now's the time. In this space provided, write about your decision to change how you love and are loved. Begin with some form of the following affirmation: *I acknowledge that I am Perfect Enough and I recognize and embrace this opportunity to enhance the way I approach self-love and love of others.*

_____

_____

_____

_____

_____

_____

_____

_____

_____

_____

I=Identify Your Fears

What fears are preventing you from loving yourself and others? Where did your fears come from? Write their profiles. Remember, you cannot master something if you don't know it well.

_____

_____

_____

_____

_____

_____

_____

_____

_____

S=Self-Inquiry

Take a look at your thoughts about who you are. I'm wonder if you treat yourself as your own best friend. What do you say about yourself when you look in the mirror? Now think back to a time when you had good things to say. Think of something positive. Do you like your hair? Do you like your smile? Write about positive aspects of yourself.

_____

_____

_____

_____

_____

_____

_____

_____

_____

_____

_____

_____

_____

C=Conscious-Level Action Steps

1. Be love. The best way to attract love, or anything else for that matter, is to be that thing. Be love, and according to the Law of Attraction, you will attract love. As I tell my clients, "Be the person you want to marry," and you'll attract someone just like you.

2. Stop *needing* love. Whenever you want to attract something into your life, the worst way to do it is to focus on how much you need it. That's a surefire way to never getting it. I know that you do want and need love. We all do. But in order to make room for it to arrive into your life, you must release the attachment you have to getting it; you must release the *need* for love.

3. Learn to love yourself by using affirmations.
   - I love myself
   - I approve of myself
   - I accept everything about myself
   - I forgive all who have hurt me.
   - I love life and experience it to the fullest.
   - I enjoy the people around me.
   - I enjoy my work.
   - I am grateful for my home.
   - I welcome and graciously accept compliments.

Now add more affirmations:

_____

_____

_____

_____

_____

ACTION STEP
MODELING LOVE

- Who represents healthy self-love and healthy love of others to you?

_____

_____

- Close your eyes and imagine that person.
- Envision how the person stands, how they walk, and how they use their hands and eyes.
- Imagine that person interacting with others. What does their voice sound like? What do they look like when they're listening? Observe how the other people react to your loving person.
- Imagine yourself standing close to your confident person. How do you feel? Can you feel their love?

_____

_____

- Imagine watching that person with their partner or spouse. What do they look like when they gaze into that person's eyes? What body language tells you they're in love?

_____

_____

- Pretend you're a human sponge and soak up the love of your model.
- Turn to the people in your vision and watch them react to you the same way they reacted to your loving person. Feel their respect and admiration, and feel your charisma and confidence. Feel compassion and love.
- Now, open your eyes.

What are your thoughts and feelings about your modeling experience?

_____

_____

_____

_____

O=Outcome Development Board

Cut out and paste photos and words that represent your model of love and words and images that represent your past success onto section #6 of your outcome board. You are creating a story with your board of what you want your outcomes to be, and that story begins with "I am . . . ". Here are some tips for choosing the most effective images:

- Use your information from your self-inquiry.
- Look for images of couples looking at each other lovingly.
- If you already have a beloved, paste a photo of that person on your poster.
- What kind of body language represents love to you? Choose images that depict people with that body language.
- If there are things (e.g., an engagement ring or a wedding chapel) that represent the kind of love you want, include them, too. Refrain from concentrating heavily on things, however.

What are your thoughts and feelings regarding your experience of completing this first section of your outcome board?

_____

_____

_____

_____

V=Visualize, with the Help of Hypnosis

USE HYPNOSIS TO TURBO-CHARGE YOUR LOVE

After you've done what you can on the conscious level to increase your self-love and attract love from others, it's time to turbo-charge your progress by enlisting the subconscious by way of hypnosis, which as always will begin with Instant Alpha Conditioning. After that you can either read the love script each time, record your own CD with the script, or listen to the "Love" CD in the Perfect Enough CD series. Just make sure you follow through so that the information is recorded in your brain. This will allow you to make the changes that will attract Love in your life. Remember you are worth it!

Let's turbo-charge your true desire to be happy with love right now!

INSTANT ALPHA CONDITIONING

Instructions:

1. Read each night, before retiring, for 21 nights. If you miss a night, you must begin again. Read aloud, with feeling. Use the word you choose to replace the longer Alpha Conditioning and let Alpha easily occur.

2.   Proceed immediately to the script for Love.

S	M	T	W	Th	F	Sat

From this moment on, each and every time I desire to attain the deep state of total relaxation, I am instantly and fully relaxed, as I am now drifting into the Alpha state of consciousness. The moment I think my chosen word _____, Alpha occurs. This word has an effect only when I use it and only under the proper circumstances. Each and every time I do use it, I am fully prepared to receive positive, beneficial and constructive suggestions, impressing each one deeper into my storage and memory facility of my brain.

From this moment on, _____ triggers deep relaxation of my mind and body. I feel Alpha occur. I feel wonderful. I feel comfortable. I am totally receptive and responsive to my own creative ideas and suggestions. I am bathed in a glow of quietness, peace, and serenity. My chosen word works only when I deliberately use it for deep relaxation to attain Alpha consciousness. Its use in regular conversation has no effect on me whatsoever. From this moment on, each and every time I desire the deep state of total relaxation, I am instantly and fully relaxed upon saying _____. Because my subconscious must follow my command, each and every time I desire total relaxation, I am instantly and fully relaxed when I think my chosen word_____. I feel a deep sense of gratification as this word programming becomes a reality. Feeling wonderful, generous, alive, and eager to develop healthy, lasting, love relationships . . .

LOVE

As I relax once more, I release every fearful experience of the past that relates to me loving myself or anyone else, and everything connected with those experiences. I find it easy to let go of my fears. I am a part of life, as we all are. We all move, live, and think, as we have a right to. Life goes on, and so do I, growing rich in experience and in capacity to achieve. My positive experiences supply me with a directness to meet the challenges of my life. All I must do is use the amazing power of my subconscious mind. I am using that capacity now to disengage myself from every negative, destructive, and harmful impression ever made upon me. They fade, fade, fade out of my life forever.

I am grateful and thankful for every experience of the past. I am now forgiving myself for every mistake I have ever made; and I forgive everyone else who may have in any way harmed me. I know that out of each experience, as I understand it, good must surely come to me. I forgive myself and move toward greater opportunity and greater achievement. I grow stronger with each experience and I am stronger than anything life can offer. I am preparing myself to meet life's challengers directly, free of negative conditioning. I am more than any challenge, for I possess the power and the ability to channel any experience into a rich and rewarding way of life.

As I do a release and clear processing with my imagination, I imagine, visualize myself at the beach. It is a beautiful day and I am safe and secure and feel totally okay. As I perceive myself at the beach there is a comfortable breeze and I can hear the ocean waves in the background. And now very, very vividly, I am fantasizing that I am digging a deep hole in the sand. I am digging deeper and deeper. When the hole is big enough and deep enough, I start putting in the hole all my negative, fear-based emotions. So now as I visualize this I am making it as real as possible. I am perceiving every detail of this movie in my mind. I am playing the role. I am playing the part and I am experiencing burying each fear in my mind. I smell the sand and the sea. I take a moment and allow this to happen in my mind, and now I have just seen my own reality. I have thrown away all the negativity and the fears. I have thrown away all the fear-based emotions. I am now open to new suggestions, which I will accept and act upon. I am now open to all the warmth, joy and fulfillment that life has to offer. I feel glad to be alive and enthusiastic about my future. I am now calm and relaxed and a sense of peace permeates my body and mind.

Now I fully have released past fears and all their effects on me. I am free, free of the past fear of love, free to be me, entirely. I accept myself completely. I am a valuable and talented human being and I am always aware of my innate worth.

There are things to be done by me that are done better by me than by any other human being. Every word, every movement, every gesture of mine preserves my unique stamp upon life. There is no one who can exactly duplicate me. I am pleased, I accept myself, and I love myself. I am grateful for my new level of understanding.

I feel the emotion of warmth spreading calm throughout my body. As I use my imagination I see myself outdoors and the sun is shining brightly overhead and I feel safe and secure. I feel the warmth of the sun on the top of my head, moving down to the tip of my toes, radiating out throughout my entire body to all my muscles, like a warm blanket of relaxation, moving down from the top of my head to the tips of my toes.

The reason I am reading this session is that I wish to increase my awareness of love and my ability to love others. I have decided that I am worthy of love and that I have a lot of love to give to the special people in my life. That's right! Good.

Now I visualize a symbol of love. The symbol of love is a circle, and each and every time I see a circle or think of a circle, thoughts of love are reactivated and work on my behalf. I allow love to flow into me, around me, and out into the world. Every cell is permeated with a glowing feeling of love, satisfying the deep longing within me, attracting love to me the gentle love of acceptance. I accept myself as a lovable person. I have the ability to express and receive love. I love others and I know that I am like a magnet building love within myself, and as the love grows I attract unconditional love to me. This process is perfectly summarized in the simple form of a circle.

I express love at the level I intuitively know others will accept. I give those I love freedom to be themselves with honor, and because that love is unconditional, they return it gratefully to me. What I want for myself, I want for everyone else, as I know that everyone is made of the same substance. We are all part of one great life. In that life we all live and move and have our own power of being. Since this is true, I forgive myself now for every mistake I have ever made. I let them be released at this very deep level from every cell of my being. I allow that release now and as I do, a new level of understanding of life begins to flow into my awareness. I am prepared for life and love living it.

I allow this new understanding to permeate my cells, to fill me with caring, with compassion, with love. I know that out of each experience I have had in life, good, understanding, and growth, has filled my awareness. I completely forgive myself now and as I also forgive all those who have in any way harmed me. I let this forgiveness enrich me. My new level of love awareness now enriches my every thought, word, and deed, and as I develop a love of giving out joy, of creation, and the satisfaction of using my inherent powers to accomplish something within me, something worthwhile is increased. That something is love awareness and it grows within. And like the sun expresses warmth, I express love, love, love to all those who come within me awareness. I radiate and share my love just by being me.

My expression of love enriches, enhances, amplifies, creates and develops people and situations. I experience a fulfillment of life, and my mature expression of love frees those I love to develop their own inner powers toward fulfillment. I allow those I love most deeply the chance to be themselves to express life according to their own potentials. Freeing them automatically frees me to be more creative, spontaneous, and enthusiastic while pursuing my own destiny. Life thus becomes a joy that I find myself appreciating immensely. As I move through life achieving, I look closely and deliberately at myself and ask, as many times as is necessary: "Am I moving in this direction with love in my heart?" When I find that love center, I move with strength and the satisfaction of knowing the path is correct for me. Love creates joy, strength. It joins others in peace, with honor. Love is my guide, my companion.

The circle perpetuates, strengthens and overflows to all who require love and unconditional caring. Love reflects me the giver. Love listens to its own inner voice. Love recognizes itself, it sees, it looks, it listens as well as hears. It touches and revels in gentle loving touch, a caress of true understanding on the intuitive level. I am feeling and receiving with my power of intention. This love is forgiving, asking nothing in return, giving from the abundance within me for now right now, love is instructed to grow and be in every cell of my being. Something of value replacing the useless tension I have now released. Something of value, love, unconditional love, left free, finding its own path, setting its own pace, traveling its own way in dignity, and uniqueness. Love needs no recognition. It simply is.

The circle reflects that love and each time I see one either inside or outside of my own awareness, the circle activates each idea presented here. I am instructing my deeper mind to allow the love within me to grow until I am able to give love unconditionally. For true giving is giving, and asking nothing in return. Love needs no recognition. It simply is. Joy is always an integral part of loving. There is joy in every act of life. When we allow the awareness of love to grow within our being, to work in love is to work in joy to live in love is to live in joy. I may not have before me the most creative and satisfying day to live, but I know that I must live it, I make the choice, and I choose to use the day in energy, enthusiasm, and determination to allow it to be the best day of my life.

I choose. More and more readily each time that I see a circle, the positive, love-filled experience. Love builds daily within my mind creating more and more fulfilling decisions. I choose from the heart, from love. Love is accepting the other person unconditionally. Realizing that today is an opportunity to change, to reflect the love, I have given out. Love is constantly watching, listening, waiting, feeling, adjusting, readjusting, and changing. Love shares, love frees, and love promotes growth and competence. Love reaches beyond where we are and creates warmth, acceptance, unconditional caring. Love is a catalyst for security within. The release of dormant energy. A gift unto mankind. Circles everywhere. Circles of love. Circles of caring. Circles are gifts. Love energy grows within me. I allow it to happen. I experience the love, the circle of love, a gift, a love imprint. I let it change my life.

This entire suggestion is represented by the letter "V" of my sub-key word "Discover." Anytime I think, say, or see the word "Discover," all suggestions keyed to this word are automatically activated, stimulated and work for my benefit.

You now have the choice to either awaken or to drift off into a normal, natural sleep. If you are going to awaken, say:

Twenty minutes. Wide awake.

If you are going to drift off into a normal, natural sleep, say:

I am now going to drift off into a normal, natural sleep. When I awaken, I will feel fully rested, calm, and at peace with myself, the world, and those around me.

E=Evaluate Your Progress

After you have gone through the entire *DISCOVER PROCESS* once, evaluate the level of love you have for yourself and for others. Do you still carry the same fears you listed at the beginning? Have you incorporated qualities of the person you modeled into your life?

_____

_____

_____

_____

_____

_____

_____

_____

_____

_____

_____

_____

_____

_____

_____

_____

R=Revise & Repeat

If you have achieved your goal, congratulations! Read the following DISCOVER Flash Cards before you retire to bed each night, and repeat the word "Discover" to compound the contents of the scripts from the **DISCOVER PROCESS**.

If you haven't achieved your goal, redo the Love Key, including all exercises, and read or listen to the script for Love for another 21 days.

I am grateful and thankful for love.	I am grateful for my new level of understanding.
I have decided that I am worthy of love.	I have the ability to express and receive love.
I am like a magnet building love within myself.	I give those I love freedom to be themselves with honor.
I am prepared for life and love living it.	I radiate and share my love just by being me.
I am feeling and receiving with my power of intention	I live in love is to live in joy.

KEY 7

PROSPERITY

FROM SCARCITY TO ABUNDANCE

"Circumstances, I make them." —*Napoleon Hill*

Do you have a mentality that says there is plenty in the universe for everyone? Do you embrace that there is no such thing as scarcity, except in your mind? Do you realize that when your mind says there's scarcity, scarcity seemingly magically appears? You can create and embrace a life and a world of abundance through the **DISCOVER PROCESS**.

D=Decide There is Abundance

Deciding that you believe in the abundance in the universe is your first, necessary step toward creating a life of prosperity. In this space provided, write about your decision to change the status of your prosperity. Begin with some form of the following affirmation: *I acknowledge that I am* Perfect Enough *and I recognize and embrace this opportunity to enhance my prosperity and decide that there is abundance in the universe.*

_____

_____

_____

I=Identify Your Fears

What fears are keeping you from achieving prosperity? List them and write their profiles.

_____

_____

_____

_____

_____

_____

_____

_____

_____

_____

_____

_____

_____

_____

_____

S=Self-Inquiry

The reality of what you want lies in this section. It is quite obvious that you have a desire to make changes in your life, but to do so you must look at yourself and examine your past success or positive experiences regarding abundance. When have you felt abundance? When have you attracted prosperity into your life? Relive one of those times in the space provided. Visualizing and thinking about past successes is an excellent way to build confidence and self-esteem. What you think about is what you become. Therefore, when you concentrate on your successes, you help to create future successes. *What are some of your successes?*

_____

_____

_____

_____

_____

_____

_____

_____

_____

_____

_____

_____

C=Conscious-Level Action Steps

1.   Educate yourself. Increasing your financial literacy is a great step toward creating and embracing abundance. The more you know about abundance, the better you'll be able to imagine and manifest it.

2.   Take in more money than you spend each month.

3.   Save the maximum amount allowable each month for your retirement.

4.   Only consider spending money on *wants*, after you've allotted the necessary funds for your *needs*, and your retirement account and your savings account should be considered *needs*.

5.   Make philanthropy a non-negotiable component of your financial plan. Remember, you get back what you put out. This includes volunteering.

6.   Whatever your beliefs are about money, label them "the past," and put them in a mental drawer. From now on, commit to positive, expansive beliefs about prosperity.

7.   You can use visualization, on the conscious level:

   •   Visualize the life you desire.

   •   Visualize your achievements, your enthusiasm, and your satisfaction for continually reaching and surpassing your goals.

   •   Visualize yourself grateful for your many blessings, including your wonderful friends and family, and your meaningful job that compensates you well.

   •   Visualize yourself paying each of your bills as soon as they arrive, and having a large, positive balance in your account after you've paid all of your bills and even contributed to your retirement account and your emergency savings account (where you already have enough money to pay six month's worth of expenses).

   •   Visualize this life of yours. Allow your imagination to create every detail. Remember, your mind doesn't know the difference between what's real and what's imaginary, so when you imagine your life, you create it.

   •   Visualize only your outcome--not the details of how you reached your goal. Why? Because if you get bogged down in the details, you tell the world that the way to prosperity that you are describing is *the only way* it'll happen for you. Imagining the process can actually stop you from fulfilling your destiny. Concentrate on the end product, and let the universe find the best way for you to get it.

8. Call your mother and/or your father and tell them how much you love and appreciate them.

9. Surprise someone who ordinarily takes care of you with a home-cooked dinner.

10. Give money to someone who needs it, and don't expect it back.

11. Be especially kind to people in service positions, such as wait staff and checkout people.

12. Release the need to want payback from those you think "owe you."

13. Practice your attitude of gratitude for the many gifts you have.

14. Look in the mirror every morning and tell yourself that all good things you do come back to you tenfold (or more!).

ACTION STEP
MODEL PROSPERITY

- Who represents prosperity for you?

_____

_____

- Close your eyes and imagine that person.
- Envision how the person stands, how they walk, and how they use their hands and eyes. Listen to that person speak. Watch that person drive their car to their home and observe them getting out of their car and saying "hi" to a neighbor.
- Imagine that person interacting with others. What does their voice sound like? What kinds of things do they frequently say to describe their career and relationships? Observe how the other people react to your person who speaks well of their life, yet isn't boastful. Observe how content and confident your prosperous person is.
- Imagine yourself standing close to the person you'd like to model. How do you feel? Can you feel their contentment?

- Pretend you're a human sponge and soak up all their prosperity and confidence.
- Turn to the people in your vision and watch them react to you the same way they reacted to the person you're modeling. Feel the respect and admiration from those around you.
- Now, open your eyes.

What are your thoughts and feelings about your modeling experience?

_____

_____

_____

_____

_____

_____

_____

_____

_____

_____

_____

_____

_____

_____

O =Outcome Development Board

Cut out and paste photos and words that represent your model of prosperity and words and images that represent your past success onto section #7 of your outcome board. You are creating a story with your board of what you want your outcomes to be, and that story begins with "I am . . . ". Here are some tips for choosing the most effective images:

- Choose outcomes that represent material wealth, but don't stop there. What else does prosperity mean to you? Does it mean a clean bill of health? If so, create one and paste it onto your board.
- Be careful with limiting thoughts such as, "I'd like to have a bigger house, but what could I possibly to do ever afford that? It's not realistic!" Forget about what you think is realistic. The universe works, and if you believe in your outcome, the universe will find a way to produce it.

What are your thoughts and feelings regarding your experience of completing this section of your outcome board?

_____

_____

_____

_____

_____

_____

_____

_____

$\mathbf{V}$=Visualize, with the Help of Hypnosis

USE HYPNOSIS TO TURBO-CHARGE YOUR NEW PROSPERITY AND ABUNDANCE

All of the above are actions you can take with your conscious mind. If you practice them daily, they will become habits, and your prosperity consciousness will begin to make it known by sending you opportunities, gifts, ideas, and support for your goals and dreams. Now it's time to turbo-charge your conscious efforts by enlisting your subconscious mind, which will help make everything flow even more easily. You can read the self-hypnosis script, record the script in your own voice or you can listen to the Perfect Enough CD called "Prosperity and Abundance". It is up to you! Just make sure you program the information into the subconscious mind.

Now, let's retrain your brain to attract to you what you want!

INSTANT ALPHA CONDITIONING

Instructions:
1. Read each night, before retiring, for 21 nights. If you miss a night, you must begin again. Read aloud, with feeling, using the word you chose earlier to replace the longer version of Alpha Conditioning.
2. Proceed immediately to the script for Prosperity and Abundance.

S	M	T	W	Th	F	Sat

From this moment on, each and every time I desire to attain the deep state of total relaxation, I am instantly and fully relaxed, as I am now drifting into the Alpha state of consciousness. The moment I think my chosen word _____, Alpha occurs. This word has an effect only when I use it and only under the proper circumstances. Each and every time I do use it, I am fully prepared to receive positive, beneficial and constructive suggestions, impressing each one deeper into my storage and memory facility of my brain.

From this moment on, _____ triggers deep relaxation of my mind and body. I feel Alpha occur. I feel wonderful. I feel comfortable. I am totally receptive and responsive to my own creative ideas and suggestions. I am bathed in a glow of quietness, peace, and serenity. My chosen word works only when I deliberately use it for deep relaxation to attain Alpha consciousness. Its use in regular conversation has no effect on me whatsoever. From this moment on, each and every time I desire the deep state of total relaxation, I am instantly and fully relaxed upon saying _____. Because my subconscious must follow my command, each and every time I desire total relaxation, I am instantly and fully relaxed when I think my chosen word_____. I feel a deep sense of gratification as this word programming becomes a reality. Feeling wonderful, generous, alive, and eager to enhance my prosperity . . .

PROSPERITY

I visualize myself as a positive happy person. I am a kind person. I accept abundance in my life and I visualize what I want and it is allowed to materialize. I expect prosperity in my life personally and financially.

I use my money wisely. I give of myself, my time, and my love. I allow my inner mind to let go of any and all past fears of money. I allow my mind to expand and see my ability to achieve my intentions easily like an eagle in the sky. I see that eagle in the sky lifting itself higher and higher as it soars in the sky. In utter silence and contentment, the wind currents lift the eagle higher and higher. Knowledge fills my mind that I too can rise above any previous limitation. I am free, free to create. I am as free as the eagle, soaring high in the soft blue sky. I have all I need to allow prosperity to happen. I have all I need to open all opportunity to attract to me through the Law of Attraction. I believe that what I can perceive I can achieve. I am honest, I am enthusiastic, I am intelligent, and I am disciplined.

I am an individual who thinks before I react. I perform all my skills with a particular purpose in mind. There are rewards to each and every one of my actions. I am able to envision the future rewards and benefits of my present course of action. I possess the skills to plan for my future success, for the success of my life. My life is enhanced each and every time I reap the rewards of my work. These rewards make me even more motivated to enjoy life to the fullest.

I imagine and see myself enjoying life on a higher and happier level. I allow myself see a large image of myself at my very best. This image is the way I want to be, it is an image of how I once was, along with how I want to me. I allow myself to have the traits of that someone that I look up to. I see all the positive ideas that I have learned and read. I allow all the positive information on how money comes to me.

I see this image of me with my life force. It is easy for me to visualize, see, feel the vibration, the color and the sound of me achieving all of my outcomes. I am absorbing this image completely. I see me the way that I want to be. This is the person that I am.

This image is the very best "me" picture. I see this image as big as I can, this me, loving me, the best me I can possibly be. I am storing this in my mind as the very best "me" image.

Now I am imagining in my mind the objects of my desire. Good. Now, I see and visualize this image of me, the very best "me" along with the image of the objects of my desire. This final image brings me pleasure and increases my motivation to achieve more – at a higher level.

The symbol for this entire suggestion of prosperity and abundance in my life is the eagle. The eagle is often seen as money. It is a symbol of greatness and abundance. I feel secure in the knowledge that wealth is mine. My inner mind obeys my commands. Through the Law of Attraction, the universe provides me through my power of intention. I desire financial success, I deserve financial success, and I receive financial success. I desire an abundant supply of money. I desire money so that I can live a richer, more abundant life of greater self-expression and greater achievement. I create the outcomes and I live them, easily and naturally.

I am a kind and generous person. I expect wealth to come to me. I use my money wisely. I give of myself, my time, my money, and my love. I am an outgoing, loving and generous person. As I seek to do more good for others, all the channels of life, people, situations, and conditions pour out a greater abundance to me. Success exists for me; I have the right to it. I express life in a full and wholesome way.

I attract money. Money flows to me easily, freely, and generously. I see myself living richly and luxuriously. My heart is open to give out. My hands are open to receive. I pay my bills joyously because it means I have obtained something of value in exchange for my money. My success is steady and constant. As I grow in understanding, I prosper. Wealth is mine now. I accept it. I am grateful for it. I am pleased with my achievements.

In my imagination, I now visualize myself as a powerful magnet, attracting that which I desire in ever-increasing abundance. As I grow in understanding, in kindness, and in generosity, my mind opens to create the means to obtain, in fantastic profusion, the things money can buy. I enjoy my success. I have a right to it. I deserve it. I share my prosperity, my abundance, and my love with others. I am open to giving and I am open to receiving. From the magnificent abundance within, gained from having served myself so well, I am free to express love, generosity, and happiness. These emotions flow freely from me, for I have much to give.

These wonderful thoughts fill me with boundless energy and enthusiasm. These thoughts bring a smile to my face, and feelings of security in my inner self. My self-confidence increases and I am certain that I will attain all of my outcomes. My ambition and the energy I stir in others is contagious. I deserve to achieve even greater success. I allow it to happen.

Commitment and persistence are everywhere in my life. My communication skills are effective. I like working with others and sharing my ideas with them. Communication is the key to me working well with others in the workplace and at home. I am an effective communicator. When other people communicate their ideas to me, I respect their opinions. I take time to comment to others and my reactions are always appropriate. The way I work with others helps me gain financial prosperity and abundance with ease.

I love what I do. And I do what I love. I love my life so much. The prosperity and abundance I obtain from my life makes my life fun and exciting. Other people notice how much I enjoy my life. I practice, achieve and maintain balance in my life. Balance between my job and my personal life happens automatically. That's right, I let it happen. Balance is the key to maintaining the success that I have achieved. My life automatically is in a state of balance.

I am a positive individual. Positive energy is infused into all that I do. I speak well of myself and of my prosperity. Others speak well of me too. I am a natural leader. People enjoy being around me and saying that they know me. My positive energy is contagious. Other people feel the positive energy that emanates from me and my life. When the opportunity exists, I praise others and others praise me.

I am open to give and I am open to receive from the magnificent abundance I gain from having served myself well. I am free to express generosity and happiness. As I relax deeper and deeper, I continue to allow my inner mind to set me free, free as an eagle in the sky. My abundance is lifting with the wind currents, higher and higher in utter silence and contentment. I possess the knowledge that I too can rise above any limitation. I am free, free as an eagle soaring high in the soft blue sky.

My symbol for prosperity and abundance is the eagle. The eagle is a symbol of quietness, greatness and secure abundance. I feel secure with the knowledge that this wealth is mine. My inner mind obeys my command each and every time I see an eagle or think of an eagle. Anchored into my mind every time I see an eagle in or out of my conscious awareness, this program multiplies in my mind. I am aware of this strong, vibrant image of prosperity and abundance that is triggered within my deeper mind and I feel secure and serene in the knowledge that I truly allow financial success to be in my life. I am a financial success.

I have a wonderful sense of gratitude for all that I am, I feel secure with the knowledge that wealth is mine and I am a financial success.

This entire suggestion is represented by the letter "E" of my sub-key word "Discover." Anytime I think, say, or see the word "Discover," all suggestions keyed to this word are automatically activated, stimulated and work for my benefit.

You now have the choice to either awaken or to drift off into a normal, natural sleep. If you are going to awaken, say:
Twenty minutes. Wide awake.
If you are going to drift off into a normal, natural sleep, say:
I am now going to drift off into a normal, natural sleep. When I awaken, I will feel fully rested, calm, and at peace with myself, the world, and those around me.

E=Evaluate Your Progress

After you have gone through the entire **DISCOVER PROCESS** once, evaluate your level of prosperity. Do you still carry the same fears you listed at the beginning? Have you incorporated qualities of the person you modeled into your life?

_____

_____

_____

_____

_____

_____

_____

_____

_____

_____

_____

_____

_____

_____

_____

R=Revise & Repeat

If you have achieved your goal, congratulations! Read the following DISCOVER Flash Cards before you retire to bed each night, and repeat the word "Discover" to compound the contents of the scripts from the **DISCOVER PROCESS**.

If you haven't achieved your goal, redo the Prosperity Key, including all exercises, and read or listen to the script for Prosperity for another 21 days.

I visualize myself as a positive happy person.	I accept abundance in my life.
I use my money wisely.	I am free, free to create.
I am honest, I am enthusiastic, I am intelligent, and I am disciplined.	I imagine and see myself enjoying life on a higher and happier level.
I feel secure in the knowledge that wealth is mine.	Through the Law of Attraction, the universe provides me through my power of intention
I desire financial success, I deserve financial success, and I receive financial success.	I am a kind and generous person. I expect wealth to come to me.

Key 8

Meaning

From Insignificance to Purpose

"There is only one success—to be able to spend your life in your own way."
—*Napoleon Hill*

Those of you who have found your purpose no doubt are comfortable with the idea. But those of you who haven't are, I'm sure, a bit intimidated. But have no fear, with a little work you can find meaning in your life beyond your day-to-day existence with The **DISCOVER PROCESS**.

D=Decide to Find Your Purpose

Deciding to find your life's unique meaning is imperative to living a life of balance and happiness.

What is the true meaning for your life? In this space provided, write about your decision to discover your purpose. Begin with some form of the following affirmation: *I acknowledge that I am Perfect Enough and I recognize and embrace this opportunity to find my true meaning.*

_____

_____

_____

_____

_____

_____

_____

_____

I=Identify Your Fears

What are the fears that are keeping you from unearthing the profound meaning that's just waiting for you to recognize it? List them and write their profiles.

_____

_____

_____

_____

_____

_____

_____

_____

_____

S=Self-Inquiry

Think about all the times in life that you felt at peace with what was going on in your life. What about that time made you feel good and think positive thoughts? Write about what makes you feel fulfilled and about the moments when you have led a life worth living (and worth writing about!). What was so satisfying about your life in your moments of pure contentment and fulfillment?

C=Conscious-Level Action Steps

In my experience, the Eulogy Exercise is the most powerful thing you can do--on the conscious level--to discover your life's purpose.

THE EULOGY EXERCISE

What do you want to be when you grow up? Who do you want to be? Let's create your future self (and by future, I simply mean not this present moment) by starting from the end of your life and working backward.

1. Relax, close your eyes, and visualize your own funeral. Spare no expense with the flower arrangements, the location, the clothes you're wearing, and the coffin, if you want one. Imagine who is there and what their faces look like. Are they devastated? Are they content? Are they the faces proud to be at the funeral of their loved one who had a life well lived and worth living? Now write what you visualize.

_____

_____

_____

_____

_____

_____

_____

_____

_____

_____

2. Imagine that five people will eulogize you: your spouse or partner, your child (real or imagined), a sibling or other relative, someone you work with, and a member of your community.

    a. Who are your five people?

        i.   _____

        ii.   _____

        iii.   _____

        iv.   _____

        v.   _____

Imagine their eulogies and imagine their faces. Hear their voices. Observe the reactions from the rest of the gathering. Do they laugh? Do they cry? Do they all reminisce about your love of life, your sense of humor, and your compassion? What exactly do they talk about? Make a list of what you think they'll say if you were to die today.

_____

_____

_____

_____

_____

_____

_____

_____

Next, make a list of what you want them to say about you.

_____

_____

_____

_____

_____

_____

_____

_____

_____

_____

_____

That second list--that, is your meaning.

3. What kind of behavior do you need to start exhibiting today in order
    to have the funeral and eulogies you desire? If, for instance, you would
    like a member of your community to say you are selfless and always
    looking to give voice to the voiceless, what would you have to do--on a
    consistent basis--to create that kind of assessment from a community
    member?

_____

_____

_____

_____

_____

_____

_____

_____

_____

_____

_____

_____

_____

_____

4. At many funerals, eventually the discussion comes around to one phrase
    that best describes the way the deceased lived his or her life. At your
    funeral, what will that phrase be? Do you want people to say, "Boy, that
    Jeanne Sullivan sure had great hair!" *No?* Well, what do you want them
    to say?

_____

_____

_____

_____

_____

_____

_____

_____

_____

_____

_____

_____

_____

_____

5. Your answer to #4 is your purpose. Now you have the opportunity to recreate your life according to that purpose. You must create objectives that will help you achieve your purpose. In other words, for people to say, for instance, that you "Gave voice to the voiceless," what actions and behaviors do you have to exhibit? Make a list of them.

_____

_____

_____

_____

_____

_____

_____

_____

_____

6. With your list in hand, it's time to make it reality. Each evening before you go to sleep, read your list and tell yourself that you are the person who gives voice to the voiceless. You are the person who does all of the things on your list. And each day, do one thing to bring yourself one step closer to becoming the new you. And in a couple of weeks or months, *presto,* you can become someone who gives voice to the voiceless.

ACTION STEP
MODELING MEANING

- Who has found their purpose in their live and lives it with passion and joy?

_____

_____

_____

- Close your eyes and imagine that person.
- Envision how the person stands, how they walk, and how they use their hands and eyes. Listen to that person speak. Watch that person drive their car to their home.
- Imagine that person interacting with others. What does their voice sound like? What kinds of things do they frequently say to describe their career and relationships? Observe how the other people react to your person who speaks well of their life, yet isn't boastful. Observe how content your prosperous person is.
- Imagine yourself standing close to the person you'd like to model. How do you feel? Can you feel their contentment?

_____

_____

_____

_____

_____

_____

- Pretend you're a human sponge and soak up all their prosperity and confidence.
- Turn to the people in your vision and watch them react to you the same way they reacted to the person you're modeling. Feel the respect and admiration from those around you.
- Now, open your eyes.

What are your thoughts and feelings about your modeling experience?

_____

_____

_____

_____

_____

_____

_____

_____

_____

_____

_____

_____

O=Outcome Development Board

Cut out and paste photos and words that represent your model of meaning and words and images that represent your past success onto section #8 of your outcome board. You are creating a story with your board of what you want your outcomes to be, and that story begins with "I am . . . ". Here are some tips for choosing the most effective images:

- The US has a history filled with philanthropists, yet some amassed their wealth in rather unsavory ways. Be careful in whom you choose.
- Philanthropists are generally thought of as individuals with massive personal or family wealth, yet some of history's most giving, loving individuals lived lives of poverty (think Mother Teresa of Calcutta). Include such humanitarians in your exploration of meaning.
- What are some objects that you feel help give your life meaning? Find images of those objects and paste them onto your board.

What are your thoughts and feelings regarding your experience of completing this first section of your outcome board?

_____

_____

_____

_____

_____

_____

_____

_____

V=Visualize, with the Help of Hypnosis

USE HYPNOSIS TO TURBO-CHARGE YOUR MEANING

Now that you've done work on the conscious level, use self-hypnosis to turbo-charge your quest for and fulfillment of your meaning in life. As with any self-hypnosis script, you must relax yourself first by using Instant Alpha Conditioning. Remember you can choose to read the script every night, record and listen your own voice, or listen to the "Meaning" CD in the Perfect Enough CD Series. It is so important to follow through and complete the whole book. I have given you so much to do... Just remember that you are worth it!

Let's work with *your* powerful subconscious, and help you find your highest Meaning!

INSTANT ALPHA CONDITIONING

Instructions:
1. Read each night, before retiring, for 21 nights. If you miss a night, you must begin again. Read aloud, with feeling, using the word you chose earlier to replace the longer version of Alpha Conditioning.
2. Proceed immediately to the script for Meaning.

S	M	T	W	Th	F	Sat

From this moment on, each and every time I desire to attain the deep state of total relaxation, I am instantly and fully relaxed, as I am now drifting into the Alpha state of consciousness. The moment I think my chosen word _____, Alpha occurs. This word has an effect only when I use it and only under the proper circumstances. Each and every time I do use it, I am fully prepared to receive positive, beneficial and constructive suggestions, impressing each one deeper into my storage and memory facility of my brain.

From this moment on, _____ triggers deep relaxation of my mind and body. I feel Alpha occur. I feel wonderful. I feel comfortable. I am totally receptive and responsive to my own creative ideas and suggestions. I am bathed in a glow of quietness, peace, and serenity. My chosen word works only when I deliberately use it for deep relaxation to attain Alpha consciousness. Its use in regular conversation has no effect on me whatsoever. From this moment on, each and every time I desire the deep state of total relaxation, I am instantly and fully relaxed upon saying _____. Because my subconscious must follow my command, each and every time I desire total relaxation, I am instantly and fully relaxed when I think my chosen word_____. I feel a deep sense of gratification as this word programming becomes a reality. Feeling wonderful, generous, alive, and eager to be on purpose . . .

MEANING

I have the energy and self-love that will enable me to begin the process of discovering my meaning. This energy is so strong and complete that I will be able to always point myself in the direction of my highest good. That's right. I will now have all of the courage and energy necessary to move towards my own highest good and I have a tremendous feeling of self-love inside my heart. As I realize this, I begin my process of self-discovery. A joyous celebration of all I am and all I become. I celebrate my own vital place inside the flow of the universe. Knowing that as I feel a part of the universe, I will never again feel alone. I know that everything that has been happening is actually part of a process enabling me to do what I have been meant to do all along. All that has been occurring around me has occurred to free me so I may find my meaning in life and in the world. I also find and create all I am meant to find and create. As I allow myself to become fully aware of this, I will be able to forgive all that has occurred. Inside this forgiveness, I find even more loving freedom. I may now go into a safe place inside myself. That's right. I find a path inside myself that leads to my own truth. I relax more with every word and I find a safe, secret place that is mine only. As I find myself on this path, I become aware of a wonderful feeling of energy that

I feel now generating inside of my body. I feel a wonderful, warm and energy moving through my body. I feel it traveling throughout my body, moving very slowly and comfortably. I allow positive energy inside my heart. The feeling moves through my heart and soul as I feel more and more comfortable. I find myself in a safe, secret place inside myself. Feeling so comfortable. Very good. Now I focus on true feeling. I allow a color-filled, positive energy to move through me. My inner self is directing me toward thoughts and images that will enable me to feel joy and happiness. My inner self will continually allow a feeling of comfort and encouragement to be a part of me discovering my meaning. And I remind myself that all that occurs leads me toward my purpose. Now I concentrate on the areas of my life that require attention. I focus on these areas and imagine a wave of energy is moving through them and allowing a sense of peace to saturate them. That's right. I am letting a feeling of harmony and balance be attached to these areas so I can explore the possibilities for my own meaning in life. I am a marvelous, self-healing mechanism and I am now actively creating my own well-being. I imagine myself outside in a beautiful garden. I feel comfortable. I notice that there are two small tables in this garden. I am relaxing more and more as I allow myself to go over to the table. On this table I notice there are two small blank books. I notice on the cover of the book; it is called The Book of Sadness. I pick up the book and imagine I am writing in it all of the hurts of my entire life. That's right. I see myself writing in all the old negativity. The despair. The issues that can never be resolved. The grief. Any other emotions, thoughts, or details of the past that might prevent me from moving freely into a happy future. That's right. I jot down the dreams I had that I never allowed to manifest. I write it all down and notice how with each entry I am making in The Book of Sadness, I feel freer. That's right. I feel a sense of relief with each notation I make. Good. As I continue when the time is right for me I then move to the next step. I notice there's a large deep hole in the ground. And a shovel next to it. I imagine myself walking over to the hole in the ground and dropping The Book of Sadness into the hole. Next, I pick up the shovel and begin burying the disappointments and negative emotions of the past one shovel-full at a time. That's right. At my own pace, I am able to let go of the past and to bury it one shovel-full at a time. It is time to finish burying the book.

Now I imagine the book has been completely buried. And now I realize during this time that I can examine the positive lessons I've learned from my past. There are a lot of positives I realize and I keep all of that information. I now consider that no matter what occurred in the past, I survived because I am a survivor. I realize, too, all the steps I took in the past have made me who I am today and that is Perfect Enough. And now the person I am today is truly a wonderful gift to the world. I am aware that I've learned positive lessons from my past, and I will now be able to move freely and joyously into the future to now discover my meaning. Wonderful. I imagine picking up the second book and noticing that the cover reads The Book of Meaning. But all of its pages are blank. There's a very important reason that the pages are blank; it is up to me to find my own meaning. I now decide to either repeat the past or to learn from it, and to take what I've learned into a brighter future. It's my choice and I am now beginning the process, now working with the **DISCOVER PROCESS**. In my Book of Meaning I am creating a roadmap with the choices that will ensure my happiness, my health, and my total fulfillment. I see myself writing the chapters of my future. I write about my meaning in life and how I will make it so. I picture myself writing thoughts that come to me, letting my inner self and the highest truths and God dictate to me. All the things I will tell myself enable me to achieve my meaning. That's right.

Now I notice on the second table there are two bags. The first bag is full of grass seed. I see and feel myself sprinkling the grass seed over the fresh, pure, earth that covers The Book of Sadness. I feel myself pressing the seeds into the ground with my bare feet and toes. I notice the second bag contains three tulip bulbs: one red, one yellow, and one violet. I plant the red tulip bulb, knowing it represents the positive love that is about to grow in my heart. Now I plant the yellow tulip bulb, knowing it represents the positive health I will continually manifest in my body. Now I plant the violet tulip bulb, knowing it represents the positive life meaning that I am discovering for myself. I am fully aware I have planted positive love, positive health and positive life in the garden of my mind. And these very things have already begun to grow inside me. Very good. Every time I become aware of my past, I have learned from it and I continually let go. I am always creating room inside myself for more love and happiness. I consider this and I feel love and joy growing inside me.

This entire suggestion is represented by the letter "R" of my sub-key word "Discover." Anytime I think, say, or see the word "Discover," all suggestions keyed to this word are automatically activated, stimulated and work for my benefit.

You now have the choice to either awaken or to drift off into a normal, natural sleep. If you are going to awaken, say:

Twenty minutes. Wide awake.

If you are going to drift off into a normal, natural sleep, say:

I am now going to drift off into a normal, natural sleep. When I awaken, I will feel fully rested, calm, and at peace with myself, the world, and those around me.

E=Evaluate Your Progress

After you have gone through the entire **DISCOVER PROCESS** once, evaluate your level of meaning and purpose. Do you still carry the same fears you listed at the beginning? Have you incorporated qualities of the person you modeled into your life?

_____

_____

_____

_____

_____

_____

_____

_____

_____

R=Revise & Repeat

If you have achieved your goal, congratulations! Read the following DISCOVER Flash Cards before you retire to bed each night, and repeat the word "Discover" to compound the contents of the scripts from the ***DISCOVER PROCESS***.

If you haven't achieved your goal, redo the Meaning Key, including all exercises, and read or listen to the script for Meaning for another 21 days.

A joyous celebration of all I am and all I become.	I find myself in a safe, secret place inside myself.
My inner self will continually allow a feeling of comfort and encouragement to be a part of me discovering my meaning.	I am a marvelous, self-healing mechanism.
I am now actively creating my own well being.	All the things I will tell myself enable me to achieve my meaning.
I feel love and joy growing inside me.	I am discovering for myself my true meaning.
I am creating a roadmap with the choices that will ensure my happiness.	I am letting my inner self and the highest truths and God dictate to me.

DISCOVER PROCESS SUMMARY

Weeks	Pages	Instructions for Self Hypnosis
Week 1	Pg: 26	§ Choose Word & Practice Instant Alpha Conditioning Script § Follow with Practicing Release & Clear Script (Nightly)
Week 2	Pg: 26	§ Say Chosen Word & Practice Instant Alpha Conditioning Script § Follow with Practicing Release & Clear Script (Nightly)
Week 3	Pg: 26	§ Say Chosen & Practice Instant Alpha Conditioning Script § Follow with Practicing "Release & Clear Script (Nightly)
Week 4	Pg: 29	§ Say Chosen Word & Practice Self Confidence Script (Nightly) § Say "Release & Clear" (Nightly) § Say "Discover" (As often as possible)
Week 5	Pg: 29	§ Say Chosen Word & Practice Self Confidence Script (Nightly) § Say "Release & Clear" (Nightly) § Say "Discover" (As often as possible)
Week 6	Pg: 29	§ Say Chosen Word & Practice Self Confidence Script (Nightly) § Say "Release & Clear" (Nightly) § Say "Discover" (As often as possible)
Week 7	Pg: 44	§ Say Chosen Word & Practice Positive Self Talk Script (Nightly) § Say "Release & Clear" (Nightly) § Say "Discover" (As often as possible)
Week 8	Pg: 44	§ Say Chosen Word & Practice Positive Self Talk Script (Nightly) § Say "Release & Clear" (Nightly) § Say "Discover" (As often as possible)

Weeks	Pages	Instructions for Self Hypnosis
Week 9	Pg: 44	§ Say Chosen Word & Practice Positive Self Talk Script (Nightly) § Say "Release & Clear" (Nightly) § Say "Discover" (As often as possible)
Week 10	Pg: 61	§ Say Chosen Word & Practice Persistence Script (Nightly) § Say "Release & Clear" (Nightly) § Say "Discover" (As often as possible)
Week 11	Pg: 61	§ Say Chosen Word & Practice Persistence Script (Nightly) § Say "Release & Clear" (Nightly) § Say "Discover" (As often as possible)
Week 12	Pg: 61	§ Say Chosen Word & Practice Persistence Script (Nightly) § Say "Release & Clear" (Nightly) § Say "Discover" (As often as possible)
Week 13	Pg: 75	§ Say Chosen Word & Practice Life & Alive Script (Nightly) § Say "Release & Clear" (Nightly) § Say "Discover" (As often as possible)
Week 14	Pg: 75	§ Say Chosen Word & Practice Life & Alive Script (Nightly) § Say "Release & Clear" (Nightly) § Say "Discover" (As often as possible)
Week 15	Pg: 75	§ Say Chosen Word & Practice Life & Alive Script (Nightly) § Say "Release & Clear" (Nightly) § Say "Discover" (As often as possible)
Week 16	Pg: 88	§ Say Chosen Word & Practice Health Script (Nightly) § Say "Release & Clear" (Nightly) § Say "Discover" (As often as possible)
Week 17	Pg: 88	§ Say Chosen Word & Practice Health Script (Nightly) § Say "Release & Clear" (Nightly) § Say "Discover" (As often as possible)

Weeks	Pages	Instructions for Self Hypnosis
Week 18	Pg: 88	§ Say Chosen Word & Practice Health Script (Nightly) § Say "Release & Clear" (Nightly) § Say "Discover" (As often as possible)
Week 19	Pg: 103	§ Say Chosen Word & Practice Love Script (Nightly) § Say "Release & Clear" (Nightly) § Say "Discover" (As often as possible)
Week 20	Pg: 103	§ Say Chosen Word & Practice Love Script (Nightly) § Say "Release & Clear" (Nightly) § Say "Discover" (As often as possible)
Week 21	Pg: 103	§ Say Chosen Word & Practice Love Script (Nightly) § Say "Release & Clear" (Nightly) § Say "Discover" (As often as possible)
Week 22	Pg: 118	§ Say Chosen Word & Practice Prosperity Script (Nightly) § Say "Release & Clear" (Nightly) § Say "Discover" (As often as possible)
Week 23	Pg: 118	§ Say Chosen Word & Practice Prosperity Script (Nightly) § Say "Release & Clear" (Nightly) § Say "Discover" (As often as possible)
Week 24	Pg: 118	§ Say Chosen Word & Practice Prosperity Script (Nightly) § Say "Release & Clear" (Nightly) § Say "Discover" (As often as possible)
Week 25	Pg: 138	§ Say Chosen Word & Practice Meaning Script (Nightly) § Say "Release & Clear" (Nightly) § Say "Discover" (As often as possible)
Week 26	Pg: 138	§ Say Chosen Word & Practice Meaning Script (Nightly) § Say "Release & Clear" (Nightly) § Say "Discover" (As often as possible)

Weeks	Pages	Instructions for Self Hypnosis
Week 27	Pg: 138	§ Say Chosen Word & Practice Meaning Script (Nightly) § Say "Release & Clear" (Nightly) § Say "Discover" (As often as possible)

Notes

Notes

Notes

Notes

Notes

Notes

Notes

Notes

Notes

Notes

Notes

Notes